As in the Days of Noah

Johannes Facius

Sovereign World

Sovereign World Ltd
PO Box 777
Tonbridge
Kent TN11 9XT

ISBN: 1 85240 182 6

This Sovereign World book is distributed in North America by Renew Books, a ministry of Gospel Light, Ventura, California, USA. For a free catalog of resources from Renew Books/ Gospel Light, please contact your Christian supplier or call 1-800-4-GOSPEL.

Typeset by CRB Associates, Reepham, Norfolk
Printed in England by Clays Ltd, St Ives plc.

Contents

Foreword

As in the Days of Noah is an urgent, overdue wake-up call to the Christian church worldwide. It is an up-to-date application of the words of 2 Peter 1:19:

> *'We also have the prophetic word made more sure, which you do well to heed as a light that shines in a dark place, until the day dawns and the morning star rises in your hearts . . . '*

If we reject the light which God has provided for us through the prophecies of the Bible we condemn ourselves to walk in darkness, not understanding what is going on around us and not knowing what lies ahead.

With incisive logic Johannes cuts through various deceptive interpretations of Scripture which would feed the self-centered materialism that dominates western culture. His uncompromising, tell-it-like-it-is approach is like a cool, keen wind dispelling the fog of apathy that enshrouds so many who claim to be 'born again' Christians.

Johannes analyses the main satanic forces currently at work in the world and exposes Satan's strategy to oppose God's purposes in human history. One of the most sinister of these forces – and yet the least understood by Christians – is **humanism**.

Personally, I found Johannes' analysis of humanism in chapter 7 particularly illuminating. He traces it back to Satan's original temptation of Eve which enticed her to partake of the tree of knowledge of good and evil. As Johannes says, 'When something not only appears to be good, but also tastes good and feels good, we must conclude that it is from God, right?'

He goes on to show how deadly and deceptive this line of reasoning can be. Yet it is the essence of the philosophy of humanism.

Although Johannes faithfully exposes the schemes and deceptions of Satan, his final emphasis is not negative. He reveals how the current pressures facing both the church and Israel are God's way of bringing forth a people for the glory of His name.

The reader who approaches this book with an open mind will not be intimidated, but rather stimulated to pursue the study of biblical prophecy for himself. He will not be discouraged, but rather challenged to a fuller personal commitment to God's end-time purposes.

Derek Prince
Jerusalem
November, 1996

Chapter 1

Without a Prophetic Vision

A well-known story goes like this: two men were working on the building of a new Cathedral. A passer-by became interested and asked them what they were doing. The first man answered, 'I am putting one brick on top of another,' but the second man had a different perspective. 'I am building a Cathedral!' he replied. The first man had only a very narrow and limited view of what he was trying to accomplish. The other man had vision: a vision of the ultimate result of his work contribution. So often the church continues its daily activity with great perseverance, but has lost the vision of God's eternal purposes for His glorious kingdom.

In the Book of Proverbs we find this well-known statement:

> *'Without a prophetic vision, the people cast off restraint; But happy is he who keeps the law.'*
>
> (Proverbs 29:18)

The normal understanding of this Scripture is that if we do not have a vision, we have lost our sense of direction. We are marching on the spot without getting anywhere. Actually the New King James points out in its margin, that it is not just a matter of having a vision which is important. It is whether the vision is prophetic or not, that determines whether we are getting anywhere. The addition of 'prophetic' to the vision is most important. It underlines the fact that the vision must be updated to where we are in God's prophetic agenda. In other words the vision must have the right timing. God is doing things today that are different from things He did in the beginning of our century or at the time of Martin Luther. To be 'prophetic' means that we understand what is in God's heart for the very hour in which we live.

In one of His discussions with the Pharisees Jesus challenged these religious people on the issue of knowing the signs of the times.

> *'You know how to discern the signs in the sky, but you cannot discern the signs of the times.'*
>
> (Matthew 16:1–3)

He was talking about the fact that people can foretell the kind of weather we will get tomorrow by looking at the sky, but they are totally unaware of God's prophetic agenda. Therefore they are completely out of tune with the great spiritual events of our time. That of course, could well be expected from people who do not know the Lord, but it should never be the case with any church or part of the Body of Christ.

No Direction

The consequences of not having a prophetic vision is pointed out in Proverbs 29:18; *'the people cast off restraint.'* The old King James version says that *'people perish.'* The meaning is quite clear: without prophetic vision the people of God are lost in a spiritual wilderness. They don't know where they are, neither do they know where to go. They are like people without direction, drifting around on the rough sea in a boat that has no rudder. That does not mean that they are not still God's people, but it does mean that they have become pretty useless in terms of serving God's purposes in the kingdom. They are like the people of Israel who were on a 40-year detour in the wilderness instead of marching straight into the promised land to do God's business.

The people without a prophetic vision have lost their way, but *'happy is he, who keeps the law.'* Here then we have an indication of what is needed for God's people, and where they can obtain a prophetic vision from. True and valid visions for God's people do not come from the exercise of any gift with prophetic utterance, nor from charismatic dreams and visions. Although all of this is good and valid it is insufficient to give the church true direction for today and for the future. The vision we need comes from a correct understanding of the Scriptures as they relate to our time. It comes from 'the law', from 'The Book'. We therefore need to search the Scriptures afresh and give heed to what the Word of God has to say concerning these last days. There is no other way for the church to find its way in these days, and to know how to prioritize its life and activities.

It is therefore crucial that God's people have a clear and unblurred focus today. Only a clear vision will provide us with direction and determination in our work for the kingdom. Jesus said:

> *'The lamp of your body is the eye. If therefore your eye is good, your whole body will be full of light. But if your eye is bad, your whole body will be full of darkness.'*
>
> (Matthew 6:22–23)

The whole point here, lies in the eye that is your vision. If your vision is in focus your life will be in full light. You will know where you are and where you are heading. If your sight is diffused or blurred your whole life is affected. You will be walking as though in a cloud of confusion. The old King James version talks about your eye being good when it is 'single'. This is exactly what we are talking about: we need a clear focus! Your eye being 'evil' must then mean that you are looking in all kinds of directions unable to decide what is of God and where to go. That is what Jesus calls walking in darkness.

Discerning the Seasons

To a clear focused prophetic vision belongs the ability to discern the season we are in. God's work is never static. It moves along certain seasons, just as in nature. Listen to these words from the book of Ecclesiastes, chapter 3:1–8:

> *'To everything there is a season, A time for every purpose under heaven: A time to be born, And a time to die; A time to plant, And a time to pluck what is planted; A time to kill, And a time to heal; A time to break down, And a time to build up; A time to weep, And a time to laugh; A time to mourn, And a time to dance; A time to cast away stones, And a time to gather stones; A time to embrace, And a time to refrain from embracing; A time to gain, And a time to lose; A time to keep, And a time to throw away; A time to tear, And a time to sew; A time to keep silence, And a time to speak; A time to love, And a time to hate; A time of war, And a time of peace.'*

It follows from this word that it is very important to know in which season we are from time to time. If God is preparing a season of breaking down the old, it would not be appropriate to try to build anything. If the season is about weeping, it would be out of place to respond by laughing, and vice versa. In the same way we should not be working to establish peace, when the Lord has set out in war to battle against the enemies. How can we ever be effective and useful for the purposes of the kingdom, unless we see what it is the Lord is doing right now? How we need to be able to hear what the Spirit is saying to the churches today!

The prophet Daniel illustrates this truth. When, as recorded in the book of Daniel's ninth chapter, he discovered that the 70 years of Babylonian captivity was coming to an end, he responded by turning to God in repentance. He prayed and fasted in a serious appeal to the Lord to implement His promise of leading the Jewish people back to the land of Judah and Israel. Actually, Daniel's ministry was the trigger starting the spiritual and political process that ultimately released the Jews from Babylon and opened the door for them to return to the promised land. Through studying the Word of God, in particular the book of Jeremiah, Daniel was able to understand God's prophetic timetable. He then knew how he could line himself up with God's heart and co-operate with Him in the fulfilment of His word.

Interestingly enough today we find ourselves in a very similar situation to the one Daniel was in. Through searching the prophetic Scriptures, we also find that it is time for the return of the Jewish people from the nations to the land of their fathers. Only this time it is not a return from a single nation like Babylon, but from all the nations to which they were scattered. It is an exodus from the four corners of the earth. Over the last decade or so this prophetic discovery from the Word of God has led groups of believers all over the world to engage in deep intercession. They desire to co-operate with God in the fulfilment of His word. Personally I have been engaged in prayer events as well as prayer trips, including some tours into the former Soviet Union. My sole objective was to plead with the Lord and to do battle against the devil for the release of the Jewish people to return from the land of the North to Israel. We actually believe that the major reason for the total downfall of the Soviet empire was the persistent prayers of tens of thousand of Christians. In the wake of the movement of prayer for this prophetic issue, many initiatives have been taken to form Christian organisations providing physical assistance to bring the Jews back by air and by bus and ships. At least parts of the Body of

Christ are waking up. They see what is upon God's heart these days and hear what the Spirit is saying to the churches in these last days.

God's Eternal Purposes

We have got to understand that the driving force behind world history, is nothing less and nothing else but the fulfilment of God's purposes. God is the God of all history, and He uses His power to form history according to His eternal purposes. For the same reason Satan's major strategy is to prevent God's purposes from being fulfilled. History revolves around God working to fulfil His word, and the devil trying his best to prevent it from happening. The whole conflict in the Middle East with Israel as the focal point illustrates this in an overwhelming way. Although Israel is one of the tiniest countries in the world, it has occupied the prime position of world attention for the last many decades. Two thirds of United Nation's resolutions deal directly or indirectly with Israel. Why? Because here the Lord is apparently busy to perform the words of His prophets, and here the devil has mobilised his major forces in order to prevent God's word being fulfilled. To see that is to have prophetic vision.

In God's dealings with Israel we clearly see the importance of understanding the timing of prophetic events. We see how the prophecies of Ezekiel chapters 36–39 are being unfolded step by step. First of all the prophet speaks about the dry bones coming together in the same place. This is the *Aliya*, the home-coming of the unbelieving and blind Jewish people from the four corners of the earth. Then the next phase is described as flesh and sinews growing unto the body. This is the natural restoration of Israel as a nation. Finally the Spirit is being poured out upon the body and it rises up as an army. This is nothing less than the spiritual rebirth of Israel. The veil will be taken away from their eyes and they will behold their Messiah and be saved. In this light God's people should be able to concentrate their efforts in lining up with what the Holy Spirit is doing in the world today.

Also, in another important area we see a great battle going on today. The completion of the great commission. Matthew 24:14 speaks about the fact that God's purpose in the last days before the coming end, is to establish a testimony of the gospel in all ethnic peoples groups. This must direct the focus of the church towards the unreached peoples, at least if she has a prophetic vision. It is clear from the context in Matthew 24, that this being so the devil is stirring up everything in order to prevent it from happening. Maybe that is what is causing the increase in wars.

> *'Nation shall rise against nation and there shall be wars and rumours of wars.'*

War has always been a means in the satanic strategy to frustrate and hinder the spreading of the gospel.

But in a mysterious way, God is taking advantage of this satanic strategy to open the doors for the gospel. It is interesting to see that the devil has concentrated his effort to keep a certain group of nations from being hit by the gospel, namely the Islamic nations. 97% of the unreached people's groups are found in what is known as the 10/40 window. This is a band of nations in the middle of the earth reaching from North Africa to Japan, basically all Muslim nations. It is as if the devil has built a stronghold here trying to keep the gospel out. He seeks to hinder the great commission being completed and the end being ushered in.

Chapter 2

For the Sake of the Elect

There is an expression in the New Testament, which can give us a further understanding of what God is after. The phrase goes like this:

> *'For the sake of the elect!'*

We find it in Matthew 24:22 and 31, where Jesus is talking about the great tribulation that will take place in the last days. The awesome pressures of persecution against the believers by the powers of darkness will be so heavy, that if that period were not shortened by the Lord, nobody would survive. But *'for the sake of the elect'* those days will be shortened. In other words, the elect is the determining factor in the formation of the historical and political events of the end-time.

For this reason, we should never believe that the world is formed and ruled by power-hungry and ambitious men. It might look that way many times, but God is the Lord of all. Jesus who is the head of all creation, has disarmed all the principalities and powers and is in full and perfect control.

Paul, the apostle, makes this amazing statement in 2 Timothy 2:10:

> *'Therefore I endure all things for the sake of the elect, that they also may obtain the salvation which is in Christ Jesus with eternal glory.'*

Here Paul reveals the driving motivating force behind his whole life and ministry: the elect! For the sake of the chosen ones Paul is willing and ready to suffer any pain and pay any price. Just like the Lord Jesus, Paul does not have the world as his focal point, but the ones that God has predestined to be taken out of this world and brought into eternal salvation through faith in Jesus Christ. Paul does not suffer for any nation or for many nations. He does not suffer for the sake of secular society. He suffers for the sake of the people of God, the Body of Christ, the church. That is not to say that we do not have any burdens or responsibilities for the world. We do. But this is a matter of right priorities. Our great commission is this:

> *'Go into all the world and preach the gospel to every creature. He who believes and is baptized will be saved; but he who does not believe will be condemned.'*
>
> (Mark 16:16)

Our task has been clearly defined. We are not to assume that our assignment is to save the whole world, but we are to spread the good news to the whole world. There will be those who will believe and get saved, but there are also those who will not believe and therefore be condemned. According to the Word of God the last category will be far bigger than the first. Jesus said:

> *'Wide is the gate and broad is the way that leads to destruction, and there are many who go in by it. But narrow is the gate and difficult is the way which leads to life, and there are few who find it.'*
>
> (Matthew 7:13–14)

It is as much an illusion to believe that the majority of mankind will be saved as to believe that whole nations in this age will turn to God. We should have the goal clearly defined, so that we can concentrate all our effort and energy to go for and to work for the elect.

This was the very heart of the Lord Jesus, when He prayed His last great prayer in the garden before going to the cross:

> *'I pray for them. I do not pray for the world but for those whom You have given Me, for they are yours.'*
> (John 17:9)

And later the Lord added this:

> *'I do not pray for these alone, but also for those who will believe in Me through their word; that they all may be one . . . '* (John 17:20–21)

There is no doubt that the dying Saviour had the elect in mind and heart, because all that He had come to do was *'for the sake of God's elect.'*

Wearing Out the Saints

If we for whatever reason, do not know about this centrality in God's purpose, then we can be absolutely sure that the devil is well aware of it. His major target is the elect, God's people, God's church. From the very beginning, the strategy of the enemy has been to do all in his power to frustrate, delay and if possible destroy God's plan for His elect, including trying to destroy the elect themselves.

In the book of Daniel, where the prophet speaks about a type of the antichristian era, to which the Lord Jesus refers in Matthew 24:15, there is this remarkable word about the strategy of the antichrist:

> *'He shall wear out the saints of the most High.'* (KJ)

In other words, the devil is deliberately doing what he can to load the people of God with burdens so that they become totally exhausted and unable to do God's work. Here we do not only speak about the burdens of anxiety, sin and condemnation. We also speak about what we could call side-tracking matters. There is a high risk that we might be caught up in a lot of activities which are not wrong or bad in themselves, but are out of line with the priorities of God. Christians have great difficulty sometimes in discerning between what is good and what is of God. The reason is that we tend to think everything that seems good must be of God. The devil takes advantage of this naïvety, to drag believers into numerous and varied religious activities to sap them of all energy. In this way he can render them useless for the real priorities of the kingdom. This problem will accelerate the closer we come to the end. This is why we are exhorted again and again in the New Testament to be sober.

> *'But the end of all things is at hand; therefore be serious and watchful in your prayers.'* (1 Peter 4:7)

According to this word, at the end-time there will be an increased danger of not taking our prayer-life seriously. Once we are unable to pray effectively it is hard to overcome. Prayer has always been a top priority in the life of a Christian, and in the end-time it becomes even more important. The enemy would like very much to see us so tired and occupied with all kinds of things, that we have no time or energy to pray.

We can learn a lot about the strategy of the enemy in 1 Peter 5:6–9. Here we are told that the devil goes around like a roaring lion seeking whom he may devour. Those he is seeking to devour are not in the world, because they are already in his power. No, those referred to here are the people of God. The meaning of being 'devoured' or 'swallowed up' is described by the previous verses. We are called upon to be sober and vigilant, implying that somehow the devil is trying to drug us so that we are no longer in control of our senses. The way he does this is through 'cares'. That is why we are exhorted to cast all our cares upon the Lord, for He cares for us (verse 5). The devil seeks to swallow us up with cares so that, overcome with anxiety, we cannot sense God's priorities, let alone engage ourselves in them.

It is interesting that Jesus also warns us against the cares or the business of this life:

> *'But take heed to yourselves, lest your hearts be weighed down with carousing, drunkenness, and cares of this life, and that day come on you unexpectedly.'*
> (Luke 21:34)

Notice that the *'cares of this life'* are likened to dissipation and drunkenness. It has the same effect of making us lose our senses, not knowing where we are or where we are going, as in the case of a drunken person. That is why we are called upon to be sober in these last days.

A Sober End-time Picture

In facing the last days we need to be sober, and we need a sober end-time vision. Otherwise we will not be able to prepare ourselves in the right way, and that could have disastrous consequences. The last days will be a time of great sleepiness and spiritual unawareness. That is the reason why Jesus compared it with the time of Noah:

> *'For as the days of Noah were, so also will the coming of the Son of Man be. For as in the days before the flood, they were eating and drinking, marrying and giving in marriage, until the day that Noah entered the ark, and did not know until the flood came and took*

> *them all away, so also will the coming of the Son of Man be.'* (Matthew 24:36–37)

The people were completely ignorant and unaware of what was about to happen. It was as if they had been drugged. They were totally sunk in the pleasures of the flesh. Only one person knew what was coming – Noah – and that was because he was able to hear God. When he heard God he believed Him, and set out to prepare for the coming of the flood. As the church of God we desperately need to be able to hear *'what the Spirit is saying to the churches.'* This is the only way in which we can prepare ourselves for the end-time battle. For much of the church today it appears as if we are sucked into the same preoccupation with the carnal appetites of daily living. To a large degree the church today has become focused on consumerism and self-centredness. It is as if we think that we are going to continue our lives here on earth for ever. That could also be the reason why so little is spoken about the second coming of Christ. In many places God's people seem to be unaware of the nearness of the return of the Lord. We need to sober up and face the realities of the days in which we live.

Having a sober end-time vision means that we are able to receive the realities of Jesus' speech in Matthew 24 and get rid of our own wishful fantasies. And there are quite a few charismatic fantasies flying around in the air, some of which we shall deal with later on in this book. Here we want to point out that since we are in the days which are as the days of Noah, we might learn a few lessons from the way Noah acted.

Noah built an ark to prepare for a safe transfer from a dying old world to a new one. He did not try to work for the salvation of the present world, since he had heard from God that it had been condemned to disappear. Instead, Noah saw his calling as one of providing an ark of salvation for everyone who would hear the warning and move into the ark. In this we see a clear parallel to our situation in the last days. As in the days of Noah so it is in the days before the coming of the Son of Man. The central issue is not about saving this present world order, because as in the days of Noah, God has judged it must disappear and give way to a new world order: the Kingdom of God! The real issue is about providing a way of salvation for everyone who will believe and receive the gospel.

The New Testament lends no support to those who believe that God has given us the task in these last days to try to reform present society or to Christianize it. Paul in 1 Corinthians 7:31 is clear about this: *'For the form of this world is passing away,'* the world here according to the Greek meaning the present 'orderly arrangement'. Paul's conviction that the world is already judged by God to disappear, and not to be reformed, is so strong that he uses it as an argument to encourage young believers to think twice before they start a family. This, according to Paul, would make them take on the cares of a temporary system.

The apostle John echoes this point of view in 1 John 2:17 when he says:

> *'The world is passing away, and the lust of it, but he who does the will of God abides forever.'*

In the light of this it is quite logical that all talk about reforming present society or Christianizing the nations, is little more than wishful thinking. Also, we have to consider that the Bible speaks clearly about an antichristian empire emerging on the earth in the last days. This will be Satan's last attempt in history to assemble the nations in a global rebellion against God and His anointed one. It is extraordinary to teach that our present society can be reformed and accept Christian values at the very time when, as the Bible prophesies, the nations will fall under the power of the antichrist. When we hear in Christian circles slogans such as 'Possessing the nations for God' or 'Our nation shall be saved', indicating that in this age we as the church should be able to conquer the world, it is a clear sign that we have little understanding of both the Word of God and the way the world is going. Individuals can and do get saved, but the Bible does not indicate that we shall take over the world. Rather, as in the days of Noah, things will deteriorate until judgement comes.

When Jesus paints the picture of the world and the nations in Matthew 24 He does not give us the option that if we as the church would make an extraordinary effort, these signs of the last days could somehow be prevented. No, the global deception, the wars, the ethnic strife, the famines, the earthquakes and the persecution of the saints will happen just as Jesus describes. The shaking of the nations and of creation must come, because it serves God's purpose for mankind and the earth. God has no plan or wish to save the present world or to preserve the present political system or systems. God has, as in the days of Noah, decided to get rid of the world and replace it with a new one called the Kingdom of God. All the turmoil this poor old world will go through in the last days will serve to prove this one point: that a world which has rejected God, His Word and His Messiah will never succeed. It is like the generation who set out to build the tower of Babel in its own strength and without God. God had no choice other than to destroy it. In the same way God has no place for a society which has rejected Him and is trying to succeed through its own humanistic power and wisdom. When we as God's people think that we can do something to improve and save this present world, we are not only wasting our time and our resources, but we are in fact contradicting God's very own purpose.

What is our calling as the church then in the last days? As in the days of Noah, it is to build the ark of salvation. That is, to work for the new world; to prepare for the coming of the Kingdom of God. We can be a testimony in this world by pointing to the one and only way of salvation. Through repentance and faith in the Son of God, Jesus Christ, who is the ark of salvation, people can be transferred from a dying world into the glorious Kingdom of God.

Chapter 3

Bringing in the Harvest

The centre of God's attention and of all His work on the earth is the elect. The 'elect' is a term that covers two distinctive groups of people in the Bible: the New Testament church and the people of the old covenant, the remnant of the Jewish people. These two groups will in the end merge into one group, because God of course has only one people. Romans 11:25–26 says:

> *'... that hardening in part has happened to Israel until the fullness of Gentiles has come in. And so all Israel will be saved...'*

Then Paul goes on to talk about the remnant of Israel entering into the new covenant. In this chapter our focus will be on the fullness of the Gentiles, bringing in the harvest among the nations into the kingdom of God. The 'fullness' here as understood from the Greek means both the full number as well as the spiritual maturity of God's people.

In Jesus' great high priestly prayer, we see the focus of God's heart. The prayer of the Lord revolves around this one theme: those whom the Father has given Him. But not only those who are already His; but also those *'who will believe in Me through their word'* (John 17:20). This is the entire harvest down through the centuries since the beginning of the church.

We find this emphasis clearly stated in Matthew 24:14:

> *'And this gospel of the kingdom will be preached in all the world as a witness to all the nations, and then the end will come.'*

As in the days of Noah, we belong to the end-time; a time of bringing in the harvest, completing what we call the great commission:

> *'Go therefore and make disciples of all the nations, baptizing them in the name of the Father and of the Son and of the Holy Spirit, teaching them to observe all things that I have commanded you.'*
>
> (Matthew 28:19–20)

Here are some things we need to pay attention to and try to understand correctly.

First of all the task is defined. We as the church are commissioned to go out and bring in a harvest from all the nations. Nations here is the Greek word *'ethnos'* meaning ethnic groups of people, not states. We have around 300 states in our world, but we have about 12,000 ethnic peoples groups all over the world, of which at least a third are unreached; untouched with the gospel of Jesus Christ.

Also, we are told to make disciples *'of all the nations.'* In this context this means taking out those from the ethnic peoples who would become followers of Christ. It is not making whole nations into disciples, but making disciples out of people coming from all the nations. This is clear from the fact that whose who are made disciples should be baptized. This is of course individuals, since there is no way you can baptize whole nations. Also you cannot teach a whole nation to obey Jesus' commandments, since people who are not born again won't and can't keep His commandments, because they do not have the Holy Spirit. The New Testament prerequisite for keeping the law of God is that you have been saved. Let me make this one thing clear. I do not believe that there is any biblical evidence that whole nations can be discipled or saved in this present age. To talk about Christianizing whole nations is an extra-biblical wishful thought. There is a place for whole nations coming under the rule of God, but that is not under this present age. It belongs to the coming millenium age of the Kingdom of God. It is a future possibility that is linked with the return of the King of the nations, when He will assume all power and authority upon the earth and will reign and rule from pole to pole. But even during that age there is no clear biblical evidence that the nations in the kingdom will be 'saved' in the evangelical sense of that word. We should definitely reject the current stream of theology called 'dominion theology' or 'kingdom now'. Such expressions of man's wishful thinking will only lead to a great waste of time and energy and in the end leave God's people in a state of great confusion and discouragement.

The idea of making nations 'Christian' is by no means new. The idea goes all the way back to emperor Constantine the Great, who invented the idea that state and church should merge and become one. This did not work in his time and it has not worked at any other time in history. Trying to bring the world together with the kingdom will always end with the world taking over. Attempts to do so have resulted in many grim and cruel methods being used to force Christianity upon people. The Crusades are just one example of this. We are not here to take any nation for God or put any nation under God. We are here to complete the taking out of the elect from every tribe, tongue and ethnic people. We are here to bring the harvest into the barn or into the ark, before God's wrath and judgment will hit the earth and those who dwell in it.

Building God's Kingdom

This gospel of the Kingdom must be preached in all the world before the end comes, Jesus said. The gospel of the Kingdom means that we are to do more than just preach the good news of salvation. We are to preach the Kingdom, meaning that God does not just want people to go to heaven, but He wants them to come under the lordship of Christ, to be changed into kingdom characters and kingdom life. That is why fulfilling the great commission is more than just rushing through the earth and its nations with gospel messages. God wants a testimony to be established in all the nations of the world: a living witness to the saving and transforming power of the Lord Jesus Christ. That witness can only be the church, a permanent prophetic voice and life to show the world the way to Christ and God's kingdom. A corporate testimony that is an embodiment of the very teachings of Christ. Jesus talked about the church being a city lying on a hill which could not be hidden. He called it the light of the world. To complete the great commission therefore means that we are to preach the gospel and plant churches all over, so that there is a permanent illustration in flesh and blood of the Kingdom of God on the earth.

Furthermore this witness should be planted in all the nations before the end comes. This gives us a lot to think about. We are to make sure that the gospel is solidly planted in every one of the 12,000 ethnic groups as a prelude to the coming of the Master. We are not, as it were, to concentrate only on our own nation in order to promote the gospel there. And we are certainly not to imagine that our work of evangelisation could bring the whole nation to Christ. We are to make sure that there is a living testimony to Christ in all communities of our nation. But more than that. We are to reach out to the unreached peoples to plant the gospel of the Kingdom there. The end cannot come just because we have a good representation of saved souls from some of the nations.

We need to gather in the elect from all the nations. And since there are still a few thousand such nations where there is absolutely no witness, we must dare to change our strategy of evangelisation if we want to speed up the coming of the Lord. Oswald Smith from Toronto, who was one of the greatest missionaries of the 20th century once said this:

> 'It is not fair that some countries have heard the gospel twice, when there are many that have not heard it once.'

The truth is much worse than that. There are countries in this world who have heard the gospel hundreds of times, whereas there are still a few thousand who have not yet heard it once. In the so-called Christian world we have had the gospel for more than a thousand years. I know that that does not mean that we have always heard the true message of the good news throughout this last millenium. However, it does mean that we have always had a true witness, however small it may have been at times, and a church, however weak it has been from time to time. As we have now entered into the last days we must consider that it is time to give first priority to the completion of our great calling. To reach out and plant the gospel in the unreached people groups before, or at least at the same time, as we are carrying on with preaching at home.

This whole understanding is also linked with the teaching in the Bible that the elect means a selected group. Nobody can deny the fact that the Word of God speaks about God having a predestined people for salvation. We might not like this idea, or we might not even agree with God, but it remains an unmistakeable fact that the New Testament speaks about predestination. There are a certain number of the elect which have yet to come into the kingdom. This is what is understood as the fullness of the Gentiles. However, since only God knows the full number and has not chosen to reveal it to us, we shall have to carry on with the preaching of the gospel in all the world until Jesus comes.

The fullness of the Gentiles does not only mean the full number. The Greek word used here can also be interpreted 'maturity'. The fullness that we are working for is not only quantity but also fullness of spiritual maturity. This can be seen from several biblical references speaking about the end-time; for instance Revelation 19:7:

> *'Let us be glad and rejoice and give Him glory, for the marriage of the Lamb has come, and His wife has made herself ready.'*

His wife having made herself ready, is a clear reference to spiritual maturity. The church is called the bride of Christ. Being called His wife, must mean that she has grown into real spiritual maturity. We find the same thought in the letter to the Ephesians:

> *'Christ also loved the church and gave Himself for her, that He might sanctify and cleanse her with the washing of water by the word, that He might present her to Himself a glorious church, not having spot or wrinkle or any such thing, but that she should be holy and without blemish.'* (Ephesians 5:25–27)

Surely when the Lord Jesus comes back as the heavenly bridegroom He expects to find the church, His bride, ready to share with Him His glorious reign and rule. Such a high calling does require fullness of spiritual maturity. One thing that certainly belongs to the maturity of the bride is the whole issue of unity. In order for the church to become a glorious church it must attain true unity. Once again we hear the words of Jesus concerning His bride the church:

> *'And the glory which You gave Me I have given them, that they may be one just as We are one: I in them, and You in Me; that they may be perfect in one, and that the world may know that You have sent Me.'*
> (John 17:22–23)

A glorious church means a church in perfect unity. No unity – no glory! Jesus is going to receive a glorious church upon His return to the earth, not just a vast number of converted people. Thus the harvest is more than getting people saved all over the world. We have a calling to work for the spiritual fullness of God's people as well.

The Word of God speaks about bringing in the harvest in the end-time. That is found in Matthew 24:

> *'Then the sign of the Son of Man will appear in heaven, and then all the tribes of the earth will mourn, and they will see the Son of Man coming on the clouds of heaven with power and great glory. And He will send angels with a great sound of a trumpet, and they will gather together His elect from the four winds, from one end of heaven to the other.'* (verses 30–31)

So there will be a harvest of the elect from the whole earth at the coming of the Son of Man.

The focal point for the church in these last days is to bring in the harvest. Jesus the head of the church gives us this challenge:

> *'Do you not say, "There are still four months and then comes the harvest?" Behold, I say to you, lift up your eyes and look at the fields, for they are already white for harvest!'* (John 4:35)

It is time to lift up our eyes and catch the vision of a world that is like a field, white for the harvest.

But Jesus is giving us more than a vision for the harvest. He also has a plan of action for bringing in the elect. You will find that plan recorded in Matthew's 9th chapter, verses 36–38. The white field is the multitude of needy people. Jesus was moved with compassion when he saw that they were weary and scattered, like sheep having no shepherd. When we observe the vast multitudes of poor, needy and confused masses of people in the world, who are living with no sense of direction in life, we often feel shocked and discouraged. But Jesus sees these masses as a ripe field for harvest, and all the turmoil and upheaval is looked upon as a golden opportunity for the gospel to reach the hearts of distressed people. As a matter of fact the shakings of the nations in Matthew 24 which will create insecurity and fear in the hearts of the people, will cause them to seek after God, and will result in multitudes entering into the Kingdom of God. When they realise that all that they trust in in this world is falling apart, they will turn to seek after spiritual and eternal values. So when Jesus considers the miserable multitudes, His response is neither negative nor depressed. He says: *'The harvest truly is plentiful!'* He sees the great potential and opportunity for the gospel. As the Lord sees the plentiful harvest, He also realises where the real problem lies: *'The labourers are few.'* The world is ready for the harvest, but the church is not! Here we find the bottle-neck that is the primary hindrance to the completion of the great commission. There are too few who are willing to be sent out as missionaries to bring the gospel of the Kingdom to the nations.

Pray the Workers Out

What shall we do then? Shall we try to mobilise workers for the harvest? No, because it is not through human power and might that we can fulfil this huge task. We should rather be mobilised in prayer to the Lord of the harvest, that He will send out labourers into the harvest.

We must never forget that God's work cannot be organised through human endeavours. It will not be done by human skills such as organisation, money or technology. It is going to take more than that. It is going to take the power of God to fulfil the great commission. This was made clear from the beginning. Jesus did not want His disciples to leave right away to evangelize. He bade them tarry in Jerusalem until they had been endued with power from on high according to the Father's promise:

> *'But you shall receive power when the Holy Spirit has come upon you; and you shall be witnesses to Me in Jerusalem, and in all Judea and Samaria, and to the end of the earth.'* (Acts 1:8)

The early church did not have modern means of organisation or communication. They had no literature, no money, no satellite television or video cameras. Nevertheless, within the first 100 years the early church managed to evangelize the whole ancient world. They had the power of the Holy Spirit. This is also our greatest need today. We need to realise that the Lord is the Lord of the harvest. He has a perfect plan for bringing in the harvest. He knows how to do this much better than us. Our need is to seek His face in prayer, that He might reveal His plan to us, and pour out His Holy Spirit upon the church to call forth workers and to anoint and equip them with the power of the Spirit to go out to complete the great commission, bringing in the harvest of the elect.

Chapter 4

Global Deception

In Matthew 24 Jesus makes an effort to warn His disciples against widespread deception in the end-time. In no less than five verses in this one chapter, Jesus touches on the subject of deception. As a matter of fact, this is the very first thing He mentions in His reply to the disciples' question about the last days. Thus we can conclude that deception will be a major problem facing the church in these last days. In the light of this fact it is simply unbelievable that some Christians do not seem to pay attention to this problem. It is as if they think that being deceived is a very remote or unlikely possibility. And yet Jesus makes such an effort to warn us.

The increased danger of deception in the end-time, derives from the simple fact that Satan's efforts will reach maximum level in the last days. Because of that, an angelic voice from heaven warns those who dwell on the earth:

> *'Woe to the inhabitants of the earth and the sea! For the devil has come down to you, having great wrath, because he knows that he has a short time.'*
>
> (Revelation 12:12)

What the devil seems to be aware of, many Christians

do not seem to take any notice of. In the very same chapter Satan is described as

> *'that serpent of old, called the devil and Satan, who deceives the whole world.'* (verse 9)

It seems to me that the main feature of Satan's activity in the end-time is that of deception. His most common appearance in the last days is as *'the deceiver of the whole world.'* One can almost call that his end-time title. When the devil is thus mobilising his deceiving spirits against the church it is incredible to hear that some spiritual leaders claim that there is no need to worry. To say that there is no reason to fear deception is to say that believers by definition, are totally immune to spiritual deception. Against such folly stands the warning words of the Lord Jesus, the Head of the church. Deception is not only very possible; it is quite likely. As a matter of fact, if God did not put a time limit on the devil's offensive, all of us would probably be fooled in the end (Matthew 24:22–24).

In Matthew 24:4 Jesus issues His warning:

> *'Take heed that no one deceives you!'*

This is a clear exhortation not to take this matter lightly, or to think that we are beyond any danger. Another doubtful piece of theology says that we should trust more in God's ability to bless us than in Satan's ability to deceive us. Therefore we should have no fear of deception when we plunge into the spiritual universe. But deception is not a matter of the respective abilities of God and the devil. It lies in another place: the nature of fallen man. The Scriptures say that the human heart is sick. We all have a potential for sin and deception, and even if we are able to trust God and not trust the devil, we know that there is no way we can ever trust ourselves. Thus we need to be on the alert constantly to uphold a healthy respect for the deceiver of the whole world.

The Anointed Ones

Jesus goes on in verse 5 to say that

> *'... many will come in my name, saying, "I am the Christ," and will deceive many.'*

How should we understand this? It cannot mean that God's people will be led astray by any person who would claim that he is Christ. We are not that easily fooled. The tricky thing is understanding of the name Christ – the Greek word, or Messiah – the Hebrew version. 'Christ' as well as 'Messiah' means 'The Anointed One'. We will not find many who would proclaim themselves to be Christ or Messiah, because if they did they would be flatly rejected by the people of God. But if anyone should approach God's people and say that he or she has a special anointing, then many believers would readily follow them. This is already happening. There are quite a few who are running around in the Body Christ claiming that they have special anointings. There are those who do have a genuine anointing, but they usually don't make such claims. However, we need to be careful when it comes to those who promote their own ministry and who claim special anointings. They are appropriating the name of the Lord and claiming that they are specially anointed ones. These self-promoting and self-glorifying persons are false workers, operating in the name of Christ but leading many believers astray. On the whole all this talk in charismatic circles about anointing, is not only over-emphasized in relation to the biblical level, but it also tends to focus people's attention on special persons instead of on the Lord. Jesus warned that in the last days there would be many false 'anointed ones' and they would lead many away from the truth.

He also warned us that there would many false prophets who would rise up and deceive many (verse 11). Now, what is the biblical definition of a false prophet? He is someone who prophesies his own mind without having heard from God, and uses the name of the Lord in saying 'Thus says the Lord'. About such people the Lord says this in Jeremiah 14:14:

> *'The prophets prophesy lies in My name. I have not sent them, commanded them, nor spoken to them; they prophesy to you a false vision, divination, a worthless thing, and the deceit of their heart.'*

When someone prophesies, he must prophesy in line with the Word of God, because the Word of God contains what God has said, and is saying. If the words of a prophet cannot be confirmed with the Bible, he is not sent or commissioned by the Lord, but prophesies only his own ideas.

In the same way a prophet can be tested by checking out whether his prophecies are being fulfilled or not. The Book of Jeremiah puts it this way:

> *'As for the prophet who prophesies of peace, when the word of the prophet comes to pass, the prophet will be known as one whom the Lord has truly sent.'*
>
> (Jeremiah 28:9)

It is sad, but it must be said that when people utter various prophecies, sometimes with a time factor involved, and those words never come to pass, then we are dealing with false prophets. This should make us fear the Lord and always make sure that we have heard from the Lord before we utter anything. It is a serious thing to speak on behalf of the Lord and that is why we are encouraged over and over again in the Scriptures to test all prophecies (1 Corinthians 14:29).

False Signs and Wonders

In the same flow Jesus concludes this part of His end-time speech:

> *'For false christ's and false prophets will rise and show great signs and wonders to deceive, if possible, even the elect.'* (Matthew 24:24)

The false christs and the false prophets would not have so much success, if it were not for their great signs and wonders. And since we live in a power-minded generation of charismatic Christians, many will be fooled and led astray by this wave of deception. For too long the charismatic church has focused on the external manifestations of the faith, while having a far too shallow knowledge of the Word of God. They are not even aware of the fact that signs and wonders can also be performed by Satan, as well as God. Therefore they take almost any supernatural manifestation as coming from God and they refuse to put it to the test. In this way many are bound to fall victim to the wiles and the schemes of the enemy.

That it is perfectly possible to perform signs and wonders outside of God is an established biblical fact. For instance, Jesus confirms this in Matthew 7:22–23:

> *'Many will say to Me in that day, "Lord, Lord, have we not prophesied in Your name, cast out demons in Your name, and done many wonders in Your name?" And then I will declare to them, "I never knew you; depart from Me, you who practice lawlessness!"'*

The Lord will recognize and accept what these people did, even that they had used His name, but He will not receive these people into His Kingdom. They are declared false, together with their signs and wonders. The reason as stated in the previous verse (21), is that they did not live their lives according to the will of God. When we as God's people, accept external manifestations of signs and wonders without asking questions relating to the character of those who perform them, we are in danger of being fooled.

There is such a thing described in the New Testament as *'lying signs and wonders'* (2 Thessalonians 2:9–12). Lying must mean that they are unreal, they just appear to be miraculous, but they are fake. As with magic, it looks as if things are happening, but the truth is that it is a bluff, and we are facing 'lying wonders'. It is incredible how often believers accept everything that goes on without checking whether it really happened as proclaimed. In this way these false christs and prophets can go on fooling God's people without being exposed for what they really are. This kind of deception fools many believers, because they do not have a concern or love for the truth. They don't bother to find out or test whether the proclaimed miracles were genuine or really happened. This is a deplorable and even tragic attitude that grows in people, because they want to be positive and not challenge what they witness. Our over-emphasis on love has led us away from standing for the truth. Love without truth is like a body without bones, and truth without love is like bones without a body. People are so afraid of testing the spirits because they don't want to be negative, but without standing up for the truth, speaking up for the truth and if need be suffering for the truth, we have no real defense against deception.

Spirits of Legalism

In the last days Satan will mobilise all his religious spirits against the church in an attempt to draw her away from the truth as it is set forth in the Word of God. The dangerous thing is that his work is so very difficult to separate from the work of God. In this lies the real possibility of being deceived. When Satan works in the church he appears to be like one of us. Paul says that he has the ability to transform himself into an angel of light. If he came in the form of a beast with a long tail and horns on his forehead we would be able to expose him more easily. If he cannot make us fall into plain sin, he will try to push us to the other extreme, to make us more holy than God Himself, to drag us into legalism. Listen to these words of Paul from 1 Timothy 4:1–3:

> *'Now the Spirit expressly says that in latter times some will depart from the faith, giving heed to deceiving spirits and doctrines of demons, speaking lies in hypocrisy, having their own conscience seared with a hot iron, forbidding to marry, and commanding to abstain from foods which God created to be received with thanksgiving by those who believe and know the truth. For every creature of God is good, and nothing is to be refused if it is received with thanksgiving; for it is sanctified by the word of God and prayer.'*

As I said earlier: if the devil cannot get us to abuse God's gifts of sexuality and food, he will try to make these gifts completely sinful, and so require us to abstain totally from receiving them and using them. Such teaching, says Paul, comes from deceiving spirits and doctrines of demons. The aim is to make us fall from faith, so that we base our Christian life on self-made religious rules. Paul does not say that those who get caught up in these doctrines have fallen away from salvation, although that might ultimately happen to some of them, but he stresses that they have fallen from the basis of faith; faith in what God did for them in redemption, to a position of thinking that their relationship with God depends on their ability to keep certain rules. And if we come under the law, we come under a curse at the same time.

> *'For as many as are of the works of the law are under the curse; for it is written, "Cursed is everyone who*

> *does not continue in all things which are written in the book of the law, to do them."'* (Galatians 3:10)

It is a fact that nobody can keep all of the law. Consequently legalism will result in a curse upon us, which will ruin our relationship with the Lord.

The enemy knows this and so he tries to deceive us into legalism. If he cannot destroy marriage, and he is certainly trying to do so, he then will discredit marriage and forbid people to marry. Celibacy which has been chosen by such believers who have received grace to live alone, can become a demonic bondage which destroys their faith in the end. If anything God created becomes forbidden by law it is a demonic doctrine. But because abstinence from some of the natural pleasures of life can appear to be a holy sacrifice, people often believe that it comes from God. When people abstain from eating certain types of food and drinking certain types of drink they are looked upon as pursuing purity and holiness or as those who already possess a greater degree of holiness. It is here that the deception lies. All such extremes are engineered by demonic powers. Paul in Colossians chapter 2 refers to legalism as being enforced by *'principalities and powers.'* These were the ones he particularly referred to when he gave the great proclamation that Jesus on His cross had *'disarmed the principalities and powers.'* He concluded His victory over them on the cross by saying:

> *'So let no one judge you in food or in drink, or regarding a festival or a new moon or sabbaths.'*
> (verse 16)

The enemy is trying to put us in bondage here by requiring of us this:

> *'Do not touch, do not taste, do not handle.'* (verse 21)

And then Paul concludes with this revealing statement:

> *'These things indeed have an appearance of wisdom in self-imposed religion, false humility, and neglect of the body, but are of no value against the indulgence of the flesh.'* (verse 23)

This is why we can be deceived. It looks so right and so good, so holy and so clean, but it is in fact without spiritual value, and those who fall into this deception are rendered completely useless for God's purposes in these last days. This is the real object of the work of these deceiving spirits.

Truth or Fables

A final area of deception in the end-time is found in 2 Timothy chapter 3:

> *'For the time will come when they will not endure sound doctrine, but according to their own desires, because they have itching ears, they will heap up for themselves teachers; and they will turn their ears away from the truth, and be turned aside to fables.'* (verses 3–4)

This word is spoken in the context of the imminent coming of the Lord Jesus (verse 1) and so we can assume that the time that Paul prophetically sees here is the end-time. In the last days there will an unwillingness to *'tolerate sound and wholesome instruction'* as the Amplified New Testament puts it. People, and we are talking about God's people, will no longer be interested in the truth. They will have itching ears. The Amplified adds *'for something pleasing and gratifying.'* Truth is not interesting, because it makes claims and is often painful. People do not want that. They want something exciting and sensational. Something that satisfies their feelings. Truth cannot provide that, so instead people are willing to listen to what here is called *'fables'*. The Amplified adds *'myths and man-made fictions.'* In other words something unreal, something from the mystical spiritual world. To say it very plainly: something occult! For that is what people are going to get if they give themselves over to fables. *'Man-made fictions'* – something that has no basis in reality, but is linked to the spiritual world. Fantasies – the product of man's incredible imagination. There are hosts of religious spirits who are mobilised in these last days to deceive God's people into all kinds of mystical spiritual adventures. All because they have turned away from the truth and have become preoccupied with their own selfish desires. God's people seem willing to tolerate almost any kind of spiritual experience, without being willing to test it according to the written word of God. In this way multitudes of Christians will be deceived and deluded in the last days of this age.

Jesus said:

> *'See, I have told you beforehand!'* (Matthew 24:25)

May we take heed of the Lord's solemn warning!

Chapter 5

Nation Shall Rise Against Nation

I believe this phrase from Jesus' great speech on the end times in Matthew 24, is the prevalent sign characterizing the situation among the nations today. The demonic monster of racism, nationalism and anti-semitism, who caused the havoc and tragedy of two world wars in this century, is once again showing his ugly face. The world is suffering a revival of racism and ethnic hatred.

The word 'nation' is, as we have already seen, the Greek word *'ethnos'*, which refers to an ethnic group of people. As we look around the world today, is this not what we are seeing: one ethnic group rising up against the other? Yes, one of the major signs of the last days is appearing on the world scene as never before. In Europe this is quite evident. After the breakdown of communism, which seems to have kept it under control, the eastern part of Europe looks like a battlefield of ethnic strife. Russians and Ukrainians are rising up against each other. The Baltic people are rising up against the Russians; the Serbs and the Croats hate one another. The Slovaks feel intimidated by the Czechs, and the Romanians are stirred up in their age-old hatred against the Hungarians.

In the western part of Europe we see it as well. In Italy the old Fascist party has a growing support among the voters. The leader of this revived 'Mussolini party' has openly declared that Mussolini was the greatest Italian statesman of this century. In Austria the right wing 'Peoples party' is supported by 25% of the voters. In Spain the neo-fascist supporters have new wind in their sails and recently were able to unsettle the socialist government. Also in France the extreme right-wing parties are on the upswing. Surely nation is rising against nation. Within almost every nation there is a revival of nationalism, and minorities of other ethnic backgrounds are feeling a cold wind blowing against them. As one who has lived in Germany for several years, I am reminded of the danger of these new signs. However small and insignificant they might seem at the moment, we need to be on the alert in prayer and spiritual warfare against these powers.

I think I have seen the depth of this evil as I have contemplated what happened here in Germany during the 2nd World War. Racism and anti-semitism cost the lives of six million Jews, as well as millions of other people, particularly Slavs. A visit my wife and I made to the former concentration camp, Auschwitz in Poland, has forever convinced me of the danger of neglecting the symptoms of racism, however small they may seem.

Our visit to Auschwitz confirmed something in my heart concerning the present developments in the world. Needless to say we were deeply moved, shocked and devastated as we spent a whole day going through this camp of death. I shall spare my readers any details. For almost two days in that courtyard of hell, all I could repeat to myself over and over again was: 'This is demonic!' and 'Lord have mercy upon us!' All the way through the visit I had the sense of witnessing something of total historic uniqueness. Many crimes have been committed in the history of war, including the mistreatment and murder of prisoners of war. But the Holocaust was something beyond this, and in a category of its own. In Auschwitz, the Nazis created a huge 'death factory' equipped with all the facilities to exterminate the entire Jewish people. Furthermore, this attempted extermination of an entire race was the official policy of a legitimate state, openly declared by its head, the Führer Adolf Hitler. This is something unheard of in history. All the hair, all the glasses, the shoes and the suitcases that still remain on display in the barracks, were going to be sent to Germany for use in a wartime recycling industry. They bear witness to the fact that this was a deliberate, systematic attempt to murder a whole race. Such evil could never have been produced by a human being. It had to be the work of evil demonic forces. It had to be the work of the devil himself. The most unbelievable thing is that this incredible evil was performed by people who belonged to the most educated, enlightened and civilised nation in the world, Germany. This is just more proof that it was the work of one of the oldest and most powerful principalities in the world: anti-semitism! There are people, even Christians who believe that this could never happen again, but let me tell you this: it could not only happen again, it most certainly will happen again! The power of racism and anti-semitism is far from dead, and in the last days when Satan mobilises all his hatred against the Jewish people we will once again be witnessing worldwide anti-semitism with severe consequences for the Jewish people. That is why we cannot afford to ignore even the smallest sign of a revival of these ancient demons. There is no doubt that the reason the Holocaust went so far was due to the lack of vigilence and prayer by the Christian church. At the time Adolf Hitler appeared on the political scene in Germany the church was not able to discern what was developing. I believe there were two main factors for the failure of the church. One was the so-called Berlin Declaration, a document signed by certain leaders of State churches, banning the Pentecostal movement by declaring that it came from Satan. Such a serious violation of brotherly love, cutting off a part of the Body of Christ, must have so grieved the Holy Spirit, that it made Him draw back His life and power from the church. In my estimation, many in the German church appeared to be blind and unable to discern the spiritual forces behind Nazism.

The Betrayal of God's Word

Secondly, liberal theology had already crept into the Lutheran church. In the 1920s, liberal theologians were promoting the idea that the Old Testament was not the inspired Word of God, but just a history book of the Jewish people, and a collection of beautiful poetry and exciting myths. Such a widely accepted view (unfortunately still accepted by many) became the background for stripping the Jewish people of their divine election and calling. This was later cleverly and brutally used by the Nazis to justify their persecution of the Jewish people, with little protest or resistance from the leadership of the church.

As we are now once again faced with the upsurge of anti-semitism and racism which is the real background for *'nation rising up against nation,'* may we as God's people not be found asleep or indifferent, but may we indeed be found watchful and sober. The whole problem of the ethnic explosion could be a very strategic moment in history. It could provide Christians with many opportunities to lead the way in acts of repentance and reconciliation, thus opening up the way for hundreds of thousands of people to be faced with the gospel of Jesus Christ. Let us remember that this was the commission we received from the Lord: to bring the gospel to all the ethnic peoples groups all over the world. In all the turmoil and upheaval when the nations are being shaken and people are being filled with fear and insecurity, the church has a golden and glorious opportunity to point people to the eternal values, and to the only One who can save them from disaster and bring them in to eternal life.

Chapter 6

Building the Ark

'But as the days of Noah were, so also will the coming of the Son of Man be. For as in the days before the flood, they were eating and drinking, marrying and giving in marriage, until the day Noah entered the ark, and did not know until the flood came and took them all away, so also will the coming of the Son of Man be.'
(Matthew 24:37–39)

This comparison of the days of Noah and the last days, tells us that human society will be in a state of total moral disintegration and corruption. The lusts of the flesh will dominate people's way of life, and there will be no awareness of the things of God. In no way is Jesus suggesting that this could be prevented by any kind of action by the church. That is why I do not believe that there will be any possibility of trying to reform this present society, and I don't think it would pay to invest a lot of energy, time and funds in attempting to do so.

The situation seems to be irreversible and in a way it has to be, because man in his rebellion against God must harvest in full what he has sown. When man has chosen by his free will to turn away from God and is unwilling to repent in spite of God's long-suffering, there is no way God can allow mankind to succeed. Therefore society must disintegrate and in the end be dissolved. We cannot hope to rescue that which God would not want to save. The people at the time of Noah were given 120 years of warning, just as long as it took to build the ark, but their only response was laughter and scorn. This is how God reasoned about mankind in the days of Noah:

> *'Then the Lord saw that the wickedness of man was great in the earth, and that every intent of the thoughts of his heart was only evil continually. And the Lord was sorry that He made man on the earth, and He was grieved in His heart. So the Lord said: "I will destroy man whom I have created from the face of the earth, both man and beast, creeping thing and birds of the air, for I am sorry that I have made them." But Noah found grace in the eyes of the Lord.'* (Genesis 6:5–8)

As it was in the days of Noah, so it shall be in the days of the coming of the Lord. Only this time there is no flood coming. What is in store for the world at this time is clearly expressed by the apostle Peter in 2 Peter 3:3–7:

> *'Knowing this first: that scoffers will come in the last days, walking according to their own lusts, and saying, "Where is the promise of His coming? For since the fathers fell asleep, all things continue as they were from the beginning of creation." For this they wilfully forget: that by the Word of God the heavens were of old, and the earth standing out of water and in the water, by which the world that then existed perished, being flooded with water. But the heavens and the earth which are now preserved by the same word, are reserved for fire until the day of judgment and perdition of ungodly men.'*

The Spirit of Babylon

In the last days, the world is destined for the fire of judgment. What is it that aggravates the Lord to so much anger that He will not continue history? It is that pride and rebellion that man has shown from the beginning in wanting to make himself independent of his maker.

We meet it first in the story of the tower of Babel as recorded in Genesis chapter 11, when the people said:

> *'Come, let us build ourselves a city, and a tower whose top is in the heavens; let us make a name for ourselves, lest we be scattered abroad over the face of the whole earth.'* (Genesis 11:4)

The spirit in the people is clearly coming through here. The aspiration is to compete with God. To build something that will reach into heaven. To make a name for themselves, because they do not want to be under God's authority. To be independent of God's ways and plans. God's plan was that man should fill the earth and inhabit it, and therefore they had to be scattered. Man's plan was to stay together and pool all their resources together in an attempt to create their own society; their own world independent of God. We call this the spirit of Babylon. As God realised what was about to happen and all the tragic consequences it would have for mankind, He decided to make an end to their plan.

When we hear today about 'One World' and 'One World Government' as well as 'The New World Order' we know, that the Babylonian spirit is alive and well on earth. The devil is still trying to gather together fallen mankind with all its creative power in a massive rebellion against the living God. We see from the first manifestation of the spirit of Babel that God recognizes the formidable power and capacity man has in being created in the image of God, even in his fallen state:

> *'And the Lord said, "Indeed the people are one and they all have one language, and this is what they begin to do; now nothing that they propose to do will be withheld from them."'* (Genesis 11:6)

When mankind is pooling all of their resources together in order to 'make a name for themselves', then it means that it is building a world not only without God, but a world against God. This is the anti-christian spirit. Psalm 2:1–3 summarizes this age-old and worldwide conspiracy against God this way:

> *'Why do the nations rage, and the people plot a vain thing? The kings of the earth set themselves, and the rulers take counsel together, against the Lord and against His Anointed, saying, let us break Their bonds in pieces and cast away Their cords from us.'*

This is the spirit of this world, the spirit of the devil working to unite the nations and their leaders, in order to cast away God's Word and God's commandments and establish their own humanistic world totally independent of the Creator. At the end of this age the enemy will succeed in assembling the nations against God as never before in the course of history. In the Book of Revelation we read about the ten kings, that

> *'These are of one mind, and they give their power and authority to the beast.'* (Revelation 17:13)

And the extraordinary thing is what is said later in the same chapter:

> *'For God has put it into their hearts to fulfil His purpose, to be of one mind, and to give their kingdom to the beast, until the words of God are fulfilled.'*
> (Revelation 17:17)

In other words, this falling away of the nations from God and His Word, is something that even God is in, because it is part of the fulfilment of His purpose. Therefore it becomes most absurd when we think that in these last days we could reform this world and bring the nations back to

God. To try to accomplish that would not only be impossible, but it would also mean that we are trying to work against a purpose of God.

All this may not seem to be good news for us. A Babylonian Empire will emerge on the earth for a period of time in the last days. However it will only be short-lived and in the very end we will find really good news, namely when the trumpet call will sound:

> *'Babylon the great is fallen, is fallen!'*
> (Revelation 18:2)

Revelation chapters 17 and 18 give us an understanding of the ingredients of the Babylonian society. It basically expresses itself in four different ways. First of all it is saturated with materialism (Revelation 18:3 and 11–13). Secondly it is full of occultism; it

> *'... has become a dwelling place of demons, a prison for every foul spirit, and a cage for every unclean and hated bird.'* (Revelation 18:2)

Thirdly it is a totally lawless society (Revelation 18:3 and 17:2–3). And finally it has turned all its hatred against the saints and against the church,

> *'... the woman* [was] *drunk with the blood of the saints and with the blood of the martyrs of Jesus.'*
> (Revelation 17:6)

One does not have to be a prophet in order to see that these features of the great Babylon are exactly those that are dominating our world more and more today.

The Demonized Society

Let us take a closer look at the time of Noah, as we find it recorded in Genesis chapter 6.

To begin with we are told that the generation living in the days of Noah became infiltrated by demons (verses 1–4). There was an interaction between demonic beings, called *'sons of God'* or the *'giants on the earth'*. It may sound a bit strange to call demonic beings *'sons of God'*, but we should remember that even Satan was counted among the sons of God (Job 1:6). There is no doubt that this mingling of demons into the generation of men caused the society to become 'demonized', which of course was the very background that made God decide to exterminate it. Thus we see here a similarity between the days of Noah and the last days before the coming of the Son of Man. Also the world today is more demonized then any previous generation that has lived upon the earth. It is not the place here to go deeper into an analysis of the present society, but I think it is true to say that the presence and the power of occultism today has absolutely penetrated all levels of this present generation.

I was shocked to read some statistics recently stating that there are 15,000 full-time workers within the occult movement in Germany today. This is far more than the number of full-time workers within the Christian church. With the massive wave of the New Age, all levels of our present society must be saturated with demonic influences. That is the major reason for the break-down of righteousness and morality in today's world. Jesus said that the days of the coming of the Son of Man would be like the days of Noah:

> *'For as in the days before the flood, they were eating and drinking, marrying and giving in marriage, until the the day that Noah entered the ark'*
>
> (Matthew 24:38)

– and this life captured in the bondage of carnal appetites of excessive eating and sexual pleasures, made them totally immune to the spiritual dangers:

> *'and they did not know until the flood came and took them all away.'* (Matthew 24:39)

We find the parallel to this in Genesis 6:2–3:

> *'The sons of God saw the daughters of men, that they were beautiful; and they took wives for themselves of all whom they chose. And the Lord said, "My Spirit shall not strive with man forever, for he is indeed flesh; yet his days shall be one hundred and twenty years."'*

And following the next verse that speaks about these demonic giants and their mingling with the daughters of men in sexual relationships, God makes this final conclusion:

> *'Then the Lord saw that the wickedness of man was great in the earth, and that every intent of the thoughts of his heart was only evil continually. And the Lord was sorry that He had made man on the earth, and He was grieved in His heart. So the Lord said, "I will destroy man whom I have created from the face of the earth, both man and beast, creeping thing and birds of he air, for I am sorry that I have made them."'*

It is clear then that the final generation living on this earth just before the coming of the Lord will be just as evil and corrupt as the one who lived in the days of the flood. It is also clear from Jesus' prophecy that we cannot expect it to be otherwise. The present world is on its way to destruction and all the prayers and godly activities in the whole world cannot prevent that from happening. All talk about turning human society as a whole back to God is wishful thinking. It will never happen for the simple reason that this is not God's plan and purpose. In His foreknowledge God declares that the human generation living in the days of the coming of the Son of Man will be just like the human generation living at the time of Noah before the flood. The logical consequence of this is that there is no way to save the present world and the nations from their destiny. They have been doomed to disappear, to make way for a new world, a new system, a new age and era, which is called the Kingdom of God. Thus all our attention and all our devotion should be directed to this new arrangement God has ordained for the time following the coming of the Lord Jesus.

Noah Found Grace

> *'But Noah found grace in the eyes of the Lord.'*
> (Genesis 6:9)

This sad story continues but now with a hope and a future for the earth linked with the righteous man Noah and his family. In this we see a most encouraging picture of gracious new beginnings with God. A prophetic picture which fills our hearts with hope. Just as God provided new grace for mankind towards Noah's family, He likewise provides new grace for mankind through His chosen people, His family, the people of God. It all follows the same pattern: as it was in the days of Noah, so it shall be at the coming of the Son of Man. New grace for new beginnings! God brings His Kingdom to bear on the earth at and through the glorious coming of Christ, His Son. He bases the new millenium Kingdom upon His elect ones, built on a foundation of righteousness and integrity, formed through a people who are walking with Him in living relationship and fellowship. This Kingdom is God's answer to the world's problems. There will be no more patchwork on the old system, but a totally new beginning with new foundations, just the way God always works as recorded in Scripture:

> *'No one puts a piece of unshrunk cloth on an old garment; for the patch pulls away from the garment, and the tear is made worse. Nor do they put new wine*

into old wineskins, or else the wineskins break, the wine is spilled, and the wineskins are ruined. But they put new wine into new wineskins, and both are preserved.'
(Matthew 9:16–17)

There is no way that the new wine of the Kingdom of God in its righteousness could ever fit into our manmade corrupt political systems of democratic or totalitarian rule. This present world order or orderly arrangement can never serve God's purposes in the age to come. What we are expecting is a complete new system of government, a kingdom ruled by a great King filling all the earth. King Jesus will then rule all of creation in peace and righteousness, and we His church, His people, are invited to share in His reign and rule.

It was said by God about Noah and his family, that they were righteous before God in their generation (Genesis 7:1). In another place it is said about Noah that he was a just man, perfect in his generations, and he walked with God (Genesis 6:9). The word 'perfect' is translated in the margin of the New King James version as: 'blameless or having integrity'. These then are the requirements for God's people, for God's church as we prepare ourselves to be a kingdom of priests unto God ruling the earth together with Christ. We should not aim at spending time and energy in the church on reforming a corrupt system, but we should give ourselves to be raised up in righteousness and be trained in blamelessness and integrity. This would be a true and realistic prophetic preparation for God's people in view of the soon coming of our King and Saviour.

Noah was called and commissioned by God for two tasks in his days:
(1) To build an ark, and
(2) To preach righteousness.

Noah Built an Ark

Noah's assignment from God in an evil and corrupt

generation was to build an ark of salvation for his family and for God's creation. That ark was to be the only means of escaping the judgement and destruction of God upon the earth. God warned his servant in good time about the coming judgement and gave him time to prepare a way of salvation. This is an expression of God's great mercy and grace. He never casts His judgements upon the earth without providing a way out for everyone who has become righteous and walks with God. Also God never judges anybody without proper warning and an offer of repentance. Noah was warned so that he could warn the people about what was coming upon the earth. It took Noah a hundred years to build the ark and throughout all those years he must have been a constant target for the ridicule of the people. We can just imagine it. In the place where the ark was built there were no great waters around on which the ship could sail. It must have looked utterly stupid in the eyes of the people to build a big ship on dry land with only small rivers as a possible waterway. And when Noah explained to the people that God had told him that at a certain time the earth would be flooded through rain, he must have looked even more stupid in the eyes of the people, since it had never rained before in the history of the earth. Before the flood the earth was watered by rivers. Only after the flood did rain become a common way of watering the earth (Genesis 2:5).

In this we have a striking prophetic picture of God's provision in the last days of this age. As in the day of Noah so it shall be at the coming of the Son of Man. God has His 'Noah', His servant, which is His body, the Body of Christ, the church. Have we not been warned by God through the Holy Scriptures about the judgments of God coming upon the world at the end of this age? Have we not been called of God to build the ark of salvation, to preach the gospel, to the ends of the earth to all creatures? Isn't there a way of escape provided by God for everyone who turns from unrighteousness and receives Christ as Saviour? And isn't it also true that the preaching of the gospel and walking with God is considered foolishness by our generation? Listen to the words of the apostle Paul:

> *'For the message of the cross is foolishness to those who are perishing, but to us who are being saved it is the power of God ... For since, in the wisdom of God, the world through wisdom did not know God, it pleased God through the foolishness of the message preached to save those who believe.'*
>
> (1 Corinthians 18 & 21)

Surely the gospel today appears to be as foolish in the eyes of our generation as building an ark on dry ground appeared to be to Noah's generation. And yet it is this foolishness of the cross that is the only true calling of the church in this last generation. There is no other hope of escaping God's wrath than to enter into the ark being built by God's people at the command of God. Instead of seeking to appease this world by offering 'sensible' ways of relating to God; all kinds of modern presentations of the gospel, which often water down the whole message to some kind of humanistic and intellectual therapy, we should return with full force to preach the whole foolishness of Christ, crucified, buried and raised again from the dead by the power of God; to preach that there is both a place called heaven, the final destination for all who repent of their sins and turn to the Lord, and a place called hell, prepared for all who reject the gospel of Jesus Christ. For without such clear preaching we have not warned the people of what is ahead, in the way God would have us do, and not doing so could make us guilty before God.

To me, building the ark speaks about more than the mere preaching of the gospel. I know for a fact that the true ark of salvation is Christ Himself. It is only as we enter into Christ and are found in Him that we are truly saved and safe. But if Christ is the ark, then the Church,

His body, is the 'Noah', who has to build the ark, to prepare it and to make it available to a lost generation. This is very true in the sense that people who need Christ and seek Christ are supposed to find Him in the midst of His people, the church. I would like therefore to consider the building of the ark as the whole package: the establishing of the kingdom of God upon the earth. The words of Paul come to mind here:

> *'For whosoever calls on the name of the Lord shall be saved. How then shall they call on Him in whom they have not believed? And how shall they believe in Him of whom they have not heard? And how shall they hear without a preacher? And how shall they preach unless they are sent? As it is written: "How beautiful are the feet of those who preach the gospel of peace, who bring glad tidings of good things!"'* (Romans 10:13–15)

Jesus is the sole Saviour, but He does not work alone. He is manifested in His church. As true as it may be that a few people have found the Lord on their own, the normal way is that people find the Saviour through His body, the church. We are the saving community of God upon the earth. Building the ark is therefore also building the church; yes, building churches all over the place, and not only building churches but building them in such a way that they reflect the true character and glory of the Lord Jesus. For when the great shaking of heaven and earth and of all the nations takes place, and people are fainting for fear and distress (Luke 21:25–26) and looking out for help, there will be one place, and one place only of peace and safety: the saving community of the saved ones! Only then will what has been built on God stand firm, as it is clearly expressed in the Holy Book:

> *'... "Yet once more I shake not only the earth, but also heaven." Now this "yet once more," indicates the removal of those things that are being shaken, as of*

things that are made, that the things which cannot be shaken may remain. Therefore, since we are receiving a kingdom which cannot be shaken, let us have grace, by which we may serve God acceptably with reverence and godly fear. For our God is a consuming fire.'

(Hebrews 12:26–29)

'And in the days of these kings the God of Heaven will set up a kingdom which shall never be destroyed; and the kingdom shall not be left to other people; it shall break in pieces and consume all these kingdoms, and it shall stand forever.' (Daniel 2:44)

'And there were loud voices in heaven, saying: "The kingdoms of this world have become the kingdoms of our Lord and of His Christ, and He shall reign forever and ever!"' (Revelation 11:15)

Noah – Preacher of Righteousness

'God saved Noah, one of eight people, a preacher of righteousness, bringing in the flood on the world of the ungodly.' (2 Peter 2:5)

'By faith Noah, being divinely warned of things not yet seen, moved with godly fear, prepared an ark for the saving of his household, by which he condemned the world and became heir of the righteousness which is according to faith.' (Hebrews 11:7)

Noah's calling was to preach righteousness, and to model righteousness with his family. He was to be an expression of the kind of life God had ordained for all the people He had created. Noah's family appeared as a sharp contrast to the kind of life that dominated society in his generation. Thus he became a prophetic testimony and sign to the world around him. It is in this sense, the Scripture states, that he became a condemnation to the world.

As in the days of Noah so it shall be at the coming of the Son of Man. The chosen family of God is not only called to preach the gospel but also to be a prophetic testimony of righteousness to the world in these last days. We are to preach righteousness, not just with our mouth, but by being a living model of the kind of lifestyle God had in mind for all mankind. This is the way God wants it to be. God has an eternal principle in His dealings with sinful people: He never executes His judgment on them without first giving them a living example of what it was He had expected from them. If they fell short and would not obey in repentance, they then became exposed to His judgement. God is a just God. On that great day of judgment nobody who is condemned will ever be able to accuse God of not having given them a proper understanding of His requirements, or a proper opportunity to repent or a proper warning as to the consequences if they chose to disobey.

It is the calling of the church to manifest God's righteousness to the ungodly world. The primary hope of God in doing this, is that people will repent and be saved. But if that does not happen it is God's secondary purpose to use the righteous testimony of the church to bring condemnation on the world. There are people in the church who think that our only justification to be church, lies in our ability to bring sinners into the kingdom of God, and if that does not happen on a continuous basis we have utterly failed. Although there can be no question that the church's primary calling is winning souls for Christ, this is still not the whole truth. Even if no one turns to Christ through the work of the church, however unlikely and unthinkable that would be, God would still need the church in the world to manifest His righteousness for the sake of being able to justify His judgements.

When Jesus spoke about the function of the church He pointed out these two aspects:

> *'You are the salt of the earth; but if the salt loses its flavor, how shall it be seasoned? It is then good for*

nothing but to be thrown out and trampled underfoot by men. You are the light of the world. A city that is set on a hill cannot be hidden. Nor do they light a lamp and put it under a basket, but on a lampstand, and it gives light to all who are in the house. Let your light so shine before men, that they may see your good works and glorify your Father in heaven.'

(Matthew 5:13–16)

Salt of course, speaks about that which strongly counteracts corruption, which works and can be felt as a fighting force against decay. Salt also works to soothe pain. Jesus refers here to the testimony of righteousness from His church which will come forth as a powerful opposition to corruption in the godless society. As God's people we are called to rise up in righteousness against all corruption and sin in every possible form. It is interesting that Jesus acknowledges the possibility of the salt losing its flavor, and that as a consequence the church becomes useless and is trampled underfoot by the world. This is a clear indication of the fact that we cannot only speak about God's standards of righteousness, but we need to possess it in our own lives. That is the reason why we say that we as the church have not only been called to preach the good news, to be the positive light of the world, which attracts and draws the world towards God through its warmth and love, and hopefully bring many into the kingdom of light. We are also to represent God's holy and righteous requirements, to be a prophetic model through preaching righteousness and living righteously, and thus become a condemnation to all who reject God.

That is why we as God's people need to be instructed and trained in righteousness and godliness in every area of our life. We are not to separate ourselves from society and isolate ourselves in our own little Christian ghetto. The salt is not to be concentrated on one spot. It has to be spread out in all of the sick body. God needs righteous people at all levels of society, not in the false expectation that they would be able to take over the ungodly society and transform it into a Christian one, but with the clear objective to raise up a testimony of righteousness, a prophetic witness, in all spheres of life, as a light unto salvation for those who repent and the salt of painful condemnation for those who reject.

We need Christians in politics, not to capture the reins of power and 'Christianize' our nation, but in the biblical hope that we can show the world what God has in mind, and thus impact and influence the seats of power to adhere to God's law and word, and to warn them of the consequences if they don't.

We need Christians in the business world. Not that we have any mandate to change the fundamentally unjust and ungodly economical structures which dominate the order of this world by the power of Mammon, the God of this age. But so that a prophetic example of how God wants people to do business in honesty and justice can be given as a foretaste of the principles of the kingdom, and as a condemnation of all the corruption and evil of business.

One final thing: God's people, the church, must be instructed and trained in righteousness in this world and in this age, for the simple reason that we have been called to join the Lord Jesus at His coming in the next age to reign and rule with Him over the earth and the nations. When the kingdom comes in its fullness upon the earth we, the bride of the Lamb of God, will join our heavenly King to rule the earth with peace, righteousness, love and justice. And as the hour is close for the coming of the Son of Man, and the hour is close for the removal of this present world order, we as God's righteous family, in like manner as Noah and his family, must be prepared and ready to take over and be God's foundation for the creation of a new society: the Kingdom of God filling the whole earth, according to this mighty proclamation:

'Alleluja! For the Lord God Omnipotent reigns! Let us be glad and rejoice and give Him glory, for the marriage of the Lamb has come, and His wife has made herself ready.' (Revelation 19:6–7)

Chapter 7

The Battle for God's Word

'And because lawlessness will abound, the love of many will grow cold.' (Matthew 24:12)

The days of the coming of the Son of Man will be marked by the greatest ever attempt by Satan to remove the Word of God completely from human society. From the beginning of time the devil has done everything in his power to undermine and bring to naught the authority of the Bible. We meet this as far back in the Holy Scriptures as Genesis 3:1–7:

> *'Now the serpent was more cunning than any beast of the field which the Lord God had made. And he said to the woman: "Has God indeed said, You shall not eat of every tree of the garden?" And the woman said to the serpent, "We may eat the fruit of the trees of the garden; but of the fruit of the tree which is in the midst of the garden, God has said, 'You shall not eat, nor shall you touch it, lest you die.'" Then the serpent said to the woman, "You will not surely die. For God knows that in the day you eat of it your eyes will be opened, and you will be like God, knowing good and evil." So when the woman saw that the tree was good for food,*

> *that it was pleasant to the eyes, and a tree desirable to make one wise, she took of its fruit and ate. She also gave to her husband with her, and he ate. Then the eyes of both of them were opened, and they knew that they were naked; and they sewed fig leaves together and made themselves coverings.'*

Here we meet the first attack against the truth and authority of God's Word, which led to such disaster in the life of the humans on earth. 'Did God really say that? Are you sure you heard Him correctly? Are you sure you understood Him correctly? Maybe it was to be understood in a slightly different way!' Doubt and mistrust as to the true meaning of God's word are being injected into the mind of the woman, and she starts questioning the literal meaning of what the Lord said. This is the beginning of what in the church today is known as liberal theology or Bible criticism, a non-stop attack throughout the centuries upon the living and true Word of God. This is the start of attempting to 'interpret' God's word instead of receiving it in its literal meaning and obeying it as such. The devil is always prepared to help us to analyse God's Word and to fill us in on the meaning of it, even when God has not given us His explanation. The chief reason for the tragic fall which caused Adam and Eve to be separated from the presence of the Lord God, was their all too quick willingness to accept the serpent's offer to interpret the meaning of what God had said. The beginning of all apostasy, of all backsliding, of all falling away from the living God, lay in falling for the temptation of questioning God's clear commandments and trying to understand and analyze their meaning. The dangerous and tempting offer from Satan is that God's commandments have been issued in order to prevent us from having great spiritual adventures, and if we dare to disobey them we will indeed have access to higher spiritual dimensions; ultimately soaring to the same level as God:

> *'For God knows that in the day you eat of it your eyes will be opened, and you will be like God, knowing good and evil.'* (Genesis 3:5)

You see, what the serpent here indicates, is that God deliberately seeks to bar you from great spiritual blessings and benefits. According to the serpent God does not want you to enjoy the highest form of spiritual life, power and maturity. All these spiritual goodies God has reserved for Himself, and by forbidding you to eat of this particular tree, He is making sure you will never get access to His world of splendor and power. What a tricky and subtle suggestion, enough to fill us all with distrust and suspicion as to the real motives of God. And because we have adventurous hearts and a spiritual craving for the extraordinary, a tremendous desire to look into all the secrets of the unseen realm, we easily fall prey to the temptation of opposing God, and question the truth of His word and the good intentions of His heart.

The Natural Mind

The beginning of all falling away from God or falling into spiritual deception, lies in the fact that it is so difficult for us accept God's word in childlike faith without wanting to know all the answers. And likewise scores of believers are fooled into darkness and deception because of their great desire to research the secrets of the spiritual world outside of the framework which is given us in the Word of God.

Paul writes these striking words in 2 Corinthians 11:1–4:

> *'For I am jealous for you with godly jealousy. For I have betrothed you to one husband, that I may present you as a chaste virgin to Christ. But I fear, lest somehow, as the serpent deceived Eve by his craftiness, so your minds may be corrupted from the simplicity that is in Christ.'*

Here we have a very revealing understanding of the principle reason for falling into deception and sin: coming away from the simplicity of Christ, the simplicity of the gospel, the simplicity of God's Word. When we lose that basic childlike trust in God's Word, we expose ourselves to deceptive powers and are carried away from the truth and ultimately from God. And when we are no longer content with the limited light we are given within the framework of God's Word, but want to explore beyond the boundaries of Scripture into the spiritual universe, we open ourselves up to occult powers and get lost in a mess of mystical beliefs and experiences. We should take warning here. There are many believers and even servants of God who started out in the bright light of the simplicity of Christ and His Word, but ended their days in confusion and utter spiritual darkness, because they could not resist the temptation to go beyond what is written. One frightening example of this is found in the book of Revelation in the letter to the church in Thyatira, where it speaks about the severe judgement that will befall those, 'who have this doctrine to know the depths of Satan' (Revelation 2:24).

Extra-biblical is Unbiblical

There is absolutely no place for what is known today as 'extra-biblical' beliefs or practices. Our whole life, our theology, our experiences and our behaviour is either biblical or unbiblical. There is no place for spiritual experiments for which there can be found no scriptural basis. This whole new idea, which in fact can be called a new theology of extra-biblical experiences, which claims that the Holy Spirit can lead us into things for which there is no biblical precedence or proof, is nothing other than modern charismatic heresy. All attempts to separate the Holy Spirit from the Word of God is an act of deception. It is a tricky and subtle move by religious and occult spirits to lead God's people away from the truth. It is the work of lying spirits. If whatever we are experiencing or doing or believing cannot be substantiated by the Word of God in some measure, we can be sure that whatever we are encountering is not a work of God's Holy Spirit.

This teaching that the Spirit can take us beyond the Word is extremely dangerous. The Spirit of God is always in line with the Word of God, and He does nothing that does not confirm the Word. We need not be confused at all about the ways of the Holy Spirit, because they are already clearly outlined in the New Testament. All we need to do is search the Scriptures. In Peter's sermon on the day of Pentecost he speaks about what happens when the Spirit of God is poured out on all flesh. They shall prophesy; they shall see visions; they shall dream dreams. And in the actual happening on that day, when the Spirit came upon the 120, they spoke in new tongues. These manifestations of the anointing and empowering of the Holy Spirit upon believers are repeated throughout the book of Acts. The same thing happened every time the Spirit fell: they spoke in tongues and prophesied. When Peter visited the Gentiles in the house of Cornelius and the unexpected happened with the Holy Spirit falling upon them even while Peter was still speaking, how were the believing Jews then convinced that it was the Spirit of God? Listen to these words:

> *'While Peter was still speaking these words, the Holy Spirit fell upon all those who heard the word. And those of the circumcision who believed were astonished, as many as came with Peter, because the gift of the Holy Spirit had been poured out on the Gentiles also. For they heard them speak with tongues and magnify God.'*
> (Acts 10:44–46)

When Peter later had to defend this event before the apostles in Jerusalem the words from him that convinced these messianic leaders were:

> *'... the Holy Spirit fell upon them, as upon us at the beginning.'* (Acts 11:15)

In other words, the same happened with those in Cornelius's house as had happened with those in the Upper Room on the day of Pentecost, namely; that they spoke in tongues and prophesied!

The Holy Spirit is always in perfect unity with the Holy Scriptures. As a matter of fact the work of the Spirit is to confirm the word:

> *'And they went out and preached everywhere, the Lord working with them and confirming the word through the accompanying signs. Amen!'* (Mark 16:20)

The Trap of Humanism

Eve was fooled by the serpent, not only by his crafty and false interpretation of God's Word, but also by her own natural desires:

> *'So when the woman saw that the tree was good for food, that it was pleasant to the eyes, and a tree desirable to make one wise, she took of its fruit and ate. She also gave to her husband with her, and he ate.'*
> (Genesis 3:6)

What we see here is probably the first manifestation of the spirit of humanism. The essence of humanism can be expressed in a brief way: it is the ability to discern between what is good and what is bad according to human nature. It does not concern itself with what is pure and what is defiled or what is true and what is false or what is right and what is wrong. Only what is good or bad as it appears to human nature, human desire and the human eye. Eve saw that the tree was good for food and that it looked pleasant, so why should it be forbidden? When something not only appears to be good, but also tastes good and feels good, we must conclude that is must be from God, right? Because God only gives that which tastes good and feels good. What a deception this is! If everything which comes from God is good in the humanistic sense that it feels good and appeals to my natural desires and appetites, and all that feels bad and painful is from the devil, then I do not know God and I am unable to find any trace of Him and His work in the pages of the Bible. I might just as well join Simon Peter in his reaction when he first learned that Jesus was on His way to be crucified:

> *'Then Peter took Him aside and began to rebuke Him, saying, "Far be it from You, Lord, this shall not happen to You!" But He turned and said to Peter: "Get behind Me, Satan! You are an offence to Me, for you are not mindful of the things of God, but the things of men."'*
>
> (Matthew 16:23)

What a remarkable revelation! Peter thought he was being good to the Lord, being nice and sweet to his Master, trying to prevent Him from walking that painful and aweful way to the cross. But Jesus describes this expression of natural humanistic 'goodness' as a work of Satan. True goodness is not that which is in accordance with human feelings, but only that which is in accordance with the will of God as expressed in His Word. This whole issue is such a problem in the church today. We simply don't know how much this spirit of humanism has crept into almost all levels of the life and the work of the church. Christian people all over the place are falling into the trap. They are told by preachers, who are either unfamiliar with the Word of God or who don't respect it for gains sake, that if it feels good it is from God. And when God's people subsequently enter into all kinds of spiritual experiences, their only way of discerning whether something is from God or not, lies in whether it feels good or not. How can we allow ourselves to become so stupid, ignorant and naïve? Actually there are a lot of experiences which come from God that feel very painful and negative. The devil on the other hand, is capable of delivering 'good' things in the sense of pleasing human nature, as well as bad and evil things. We can only be sure that we are experiencing God and His goodness as long as we are moving in strict accordance with the guide-lines and the framework of God's holy Word.

Listen to this sobering word by the apostle James:

> *'But the wisdom that is from above if first pure, then peaceable, gentle, willing to yield, full of mercy and good fruits, without partiality and without hypocrisy.'*
> (James 3:17)

Notice that the first and foremost quality of godly wisdom is purity, not love, gentleness or goodness, but purity of truth and doctrine. We are to determine and test whether this wisdom falls in line with the truth set forth in the Word of God; that Word which is seven times tried and purified by fire.

The Spirit of Antichrist

The Lord Jesus in His speech in Matthew 24 points out that the days of the coming of the Son of Man will be marked by widespread lawlessness. Lawlessness will be ever-increasing till it reaches its fullness in the manifestation of 'the lawless one', the antichrist (Matthew 24:12 & 15).

What is lawlessness? It is simply the total abandoning of God's Word. God's Word is the law, and lawlessness must therefore mean the removal or the breaking of God's Word. This process is of course, nothing new. It has been the aim of the devil since the beginning, but in the end-time it will increase and become the norm in human society. The frightening thing is that this does not only happen in secular society, but the church is also being invaded by the spirit of lawlessness. As far as the church is concerned, we have particularly seen the trend of lawlessness during this century, beginning with the emergence of liberal theology in Germany in the early part of the century. One major step by this apostate movement was the rejection of the Old Testament as being the divinely inspired Word of God. Only the New Testament could – according to liberal theology – be considered to be God's Word, with binding authority for the church. The Old Testament was nothing more than beautiful poetry and myths and of course the record of Jewish history. This new study in lawless theology was to have catastrophic consequences for the Jewish people. The demonic monster called Adolf Hitler and his evil Nazi movement, cleverly benefited from this new theology, and Hitler knew how to make use of it to justify his hatred against the Jews. For if the Old Testament is nothing more than a mere history book about the Jewish people and is no longer God's holy and divinely inspired word, then God has no further plans with the Jews. They are no longer His chosen people. If they ever were they are no longer. They were abandoned by God when in rebellion to Him they murdered His Son, and since then they are given over to destruction and eternal punishment. Killing the Jews would appear to be almost a service to God and to humanity, just as Saul before his conversion, believed he was doing God's work in killing the Christians. We see here a frightening example of the tragic consequences of abandoning the Bible as God's true and living Word. Furthermore, if the Old Testament is not God's Word, then the early preachers had nothing to preach from. When Peter the apostle preached so powerfully on the day of Pentecost with the result of 3000 conversions, he preached the gospel out of the Old Testament for the simple reason that there was no New Testament yet to preach from. And when Paul travelled the ancient world and proved by the Scriptures that Jesus is the Christ, the Messiah who was promised, he did it all from the Old Testament.

Sad to say, we have seen many attacks upon the New

Testament later in the history of the church, which questions the divine inspiration of some major issues. We have seen bishops of Protestant churches deny the virgin-birth of the Saviour, the reality of the resurrection and the miracles that Jesus performed. In addition to that, major parts of the institutional church are now disregarding what the New Testament has to say about homosexuality and abortion and the qualifications for priesthood etc. Recently a major Protestant denomination at its annual synod, seriously debated whether to take the doctrine about the existence of hell out of its teaching. Hell, it was claimed, is too negative a thing to have and it contradicts Christian love.

And when it comes to the subject of the Jews and of Israel, there are parts of the evangelical and the charismatic movement who while not exactly having erased the scriptures about God's ancient people, have manipulated them into being no longer about Israel but about the church. This kind of falling away from Scripture is called 'replacement theology'.

All this and much more can only be named as the work of the spirit of lawlessness, however horrifying it may sound.

What is the biblical characteristic of the work of the spirit of antichrist?

If we turn to the Old Testament we have a clear reference to the antichristian spirit working in the world in Psalm 2:1–3:

> *'Why do the nations rage, and the people plot a vain thing? The kings of the earth set themselves, and the rulers take counsel together, against the Lord and His anointed, saying: "Let us break Their bonds in pieces and cast away Their cords from us."'*

The real objective of this global international antichristian rebellion against the Lord, His Son and all His purposes is very clear: 'Let us break Their bonds and cast away Their cords!' It is nothing more or less than total war against God's commandments and God's Holy Word, which is seen and felt as an intolerable bondage for the lawless nature of godless people in the grip of the spirit of the antichrist. The spirit of antichrist will not rest until he has got rid of the authority and influence of God's Word on all levels of human life.

In 2 Thessalonians 2:3 the Word of God calls the antichrist 'the lawless one' and Paul goes on writing about the goal of the antichrist to take God's position and place. But before he can reach that place there is something which must be taken out, because it is in the way of the full manifestation of the lawless one. I would like to suggest that the One who is in the way, is the Holy Spirit in the Body of Christ. I can see no other body in the world in the last days but the spirit-filled and faithful body of Christ, who have the opportunity of slowing the advance of the lawless one. But the prerequisite of that, of course, would be that God's people stand for the truth and the authority of God's Word at all costs. How wonderful it is to know that when the lawless one is revealed at the end it is only to be destroyed with the *'breath of Christ's mouth and with the brightness of His coming'* (2 Thessalonians 2:8).

The thing to be aware of in this connection, comes with this solemn warning from the same passage:

> *'The coming of the lawless one is according to the working of Satan, with all power, signs, and lying wonders, and with all unrighteous deception among whose who perish, because they did not receive the love of the truth, that they might be saved.'*
>
> (2 Thessalonians 2:9–10)

Lying Wonders

It needs to be said over and over again: just because there are signs and wonders it does not always mean that God must be at work. The devil is capable of performing his own signs and wonders. Their characteristic is that while appearing to be of great effect, nothing of value is happening at all. That is what is meant by 'lying wonders'. If there is no real change in the person's life who encounters a wonder, then that is a 'lying wonder'. For example, if there is great outward and emotional effect when a sick person encounters the power, but there is no healing of his sickness, then we are witnessing a 'lying wonder'. All Satan's works are accompanied with great and spectacular fireworks, but they are totally empty. The only thing that can preserve and save us from this tricky and subtle thing is a profound love for the truth of God's Word deep down in our hearts. If we 'forget' or are simply unwilling to test what is happening by measuring it against the truth of God's Word we don't stand a chance of avoiding deception. It is in the emotional area that the devil operates best. Emotions can give you the feeling that you have encountered the Holy Spirit and met with God, but such feelings can be gone in a brief span of time, and if there is no permanent change, no permanent release, no on-going fullness of new love, no real healing of the sickness, all I can say is that in that case, we are faced with a counterfeit. It is no true wonder, but a lying one, a fake one. In the same way we must be able to substantiate what is going one with the testimony of God's unfailing and true Word. If the wonder has no precedence, no root in the biblical revelation of how God does His work and what are the true signs that prove it, we would do well to reject the whole thing and dismiss it in the name of the Lord.

In connection with supernatural experiences one often hears that the people involved have received more love. May I humbly say, that that is no proof in itself at all. It could be nothing but a soulish emotional feeling of love, but that is not God's love. The real biblical evidence of somebody loving God is not found in the emotions of the soul. It is found in an obedient act of one's will. What is it to love God? Let the Lord Jesus Himself answer that question:

> *'If you love Me, keep My commandments!'*
> (John 14:15)

True love for God is manifested only in this way, that we are true to His word and eager to obey it.

Let the apostle whom Jesus loved, and who loved the Lord back in an intimate way confirm it:

> *'For this is the love of God, that we keep His commandments. And His commandments are not burdensome.'*
> (1 John 5:3)

The Authority of God's Word

What does God say about His own Word? And what does the Bible say about the Bible? It is of course of tremendous importance to know that.

In His sermon on the mount we find this statement by the Lord Jesus:

> *'Do not think that I came to destroy the Law and the Prophets. I did not come to destroy but to fulfil. For assuredly, I say to you, till heaven and earth pass away, one jot or one tittle will by no means pass from the Law till all is fulfilled. Whoever therefore breaks one of the least of these commandments, and teaches men so, shall be called least in the kingdom of heaven; but whoever does and teaches them, he shall be called great in the kingdom of heaven.'* (Matthew 5:17–19)

A jot is the smallest letter in a Hebrew word, and a tittle is the smallest stroke in a Hebrew letter!

Can it be said more clearly? The authority of God's Word carries more weight than heaven and earth put together, and every bit of God's Word will stand even if heaven and earth pass away. How dare we fiddle with it, let alone ignore parts of it? Jesus speaks here about the Law and the Prophets and together they constitute what we know as the Old Testament! How can anybody get such a foolish idea, that the Old Testament is not God's divinely inspired and holy word?

If after all we dare to challenge the truth and authority we are faced with an awesome warning from God:

> *'For I testify to everyone who hears the words of the prophecy of this book: If anyone adds to these things, God will add to him the plagues that are written in this book; and if anyone takes away from the words of the book of this prophecy, God shall take away his part from the Book of Life, from the holy city, and from the things which are written in this book.'*
>
> (Revelation 22:18–19)

Chapter 8

Back to the Cross

In view of the strong spirit of deception that would seek to attack the church in the days at the coming of the Son of Man, it is crucial that we return to the Scriptures, to the simplicity which is in Christ, to the centrality of the cross of Jesus Christ. For without strong foundations, our Christian house is not going to make it through the storm. It is a most solemn picture of the realities of the last days that Jesus gives us as a conclusion of His sermon on the mount:

> *'Therefore whoever hears these sayings of Mine, and does them, I will liken him to a wise man who built his house on the rock; and the rain descended, the floods came, and the winds blew and beat on that house, and it did not fall, for it was founded on the rock. But everyone who hears these sayings of Mine, and does not do them, will be like a foolish man who built his house on the sand; and the rain descended, the floods came, and the winds blew and beat on that house, and it fell. And great was its fall.'* (Matthew 7:24–27)

Notice that the Lord spoke this warning in the context of those who had prophesied in His name, cast out demons in His name and done many wonders in His name.

But Jesus did not know them. He did not recognize them as His true disciples. And He dismissed them with a word of strong rebuke: *'Depart from Me, you who practice lawlessness!'* He had just underlined what is important: not to be able to say Lord, Lord, but to do the will of His heavenly Father. (Matthew 7:21–23). From that we must understand that unless we submit to the authority of His will as it is set forth in His Word, we risk missing the boat even with all of our supernatural experiences. If the Word of God is not our highest authority so that we obey it and align all that we are doing and experiencing in accordance with it, we are practising lawlessness.

When you take a look at the two houses in Jesus' parable, you will not be able to find any difference from the outside. They look exactly the same. The crucial difference cannot be seen. It is hidden underneath in the ground. This speaks to us about foundations. Are we building on the right foundations? Is the Word of God, the simplicity which is in Christ and the centrality of the cross of Jesus our sole foundation?

Like the generation at the time of Jesus, we are also taken up a lot with 'signs and wonders'. There has never been a generation in the church who was so 'power-minded' as ours. That is of course particularly true about the charismatic church. We hear about 'power-evangelism', 'power-worship', 'power-praying'. Also the air is filled with the word 'explosion', which is being added to almost anything. There is of course a need to get away from the weak and feeble church and to be endued with power from on high if we are ever going to be able to fulfil our calling. But when the 'power' becomes our focus and centre of attention, we are in real danger.

In the days of Jesus they also wanted to know about signs from heaven. But Jesus warned them:

> *'An evil and adulterous generation seeks after a sign, and no sign will be given to it except the sign of the prophet Jonah. For as Jonah was three nights in*

> *the belly of the great fish, so will the Son of Man be three days and three nights in the heart of the earth.'*

The following verses are most revealing for all us 'power-minded' people:

> *'The men of Nineveh will rise up in judgment with this generation and condemn it, because they repented at the preaching of Jonah; and indeed a greater than Jonah is here. The queen of the South will rise up in judgment with this generation and condemn it, for she came from the ends of the earth to hear the wisdom of Solomon; and indeed a greater than Solomon is here.'*
> (Matthew 12:41–42)

The Foolishness of Preaching

What the Lord Jesus is saying clearly here, is that we should not be seeking the extraordinary, the sensational, the external signs, but understand that the saving power of God is centred in the finished work of Jesus on the cross, in the preaching of the word of the gospel, in the wisdom of the teachings of the Word of God. This is where our heart should be and our whole focus of attention. God is unwilling to give us any other focus, whereby we might be drawn to Him.

It makes me sick to hear how in some charismatic circles the church is working on getting rid of the preaching of the work of the cross, and to replace it with comedies and theatre-plays. The philosophy is that modern people are no longer attracted to the church, because what goes on there is too boring; it is too negative. People want to be entertained and to have a good laugh; not to be hit by something unpleasant which might disturb their spiritual sleep, wake them up and cause them to fall down before God in repentance. They don't want to hear about sin and judgment and hell, or the cost of following Jesus and becoming His disciple. They don't want to be dragged into the hard work of persevering prayer let alone fasting. No, no, no! They want to feel good and to have a good time in church. So we give people what they want. This was exactly what one leader of a megachurch said when he was asked why they had replaced the preaching of the Word with good Christian comedies. 'Because this is what people want,' he said, 'and since we made that change we have a full church on Sunday.' In a television report on this new wave in modern churches, a fairly traditional reformed church was visited. That church was only one third full for the Sunday morning service. Asked why he did not change the preaching of the Word into a humorous comedy show in order to make people feel good and thus get a full house, the reformed priest answered: 'I am not at all convinced from the Word of God that the idea of being in church is to feel good and happy. On the contrary I believe that God often wants us to be sorry and to repent when we are confronted with His Word.' And how true this is!

We are no different and no better than the crowd who followed Jesus as recorded in the Gospels. As long as they could watch the Lord performing His miracles, and as long as they could get food to eat from His great wonders they rushed after Him wherever He went. But the minute He started to talk to them about discipleship, giving up their own lives, putting down their selfish desires and come and follow Him, living a life in utter dependency of His will, this is how they responded:

> *'Therefore many of His disciples, when they heard this, said, "This is a hard saying; who can understand it?"'*
>
> (John 6:60)

And when Jesus further challenged them to lay down the life of the flesh, and to start walking in the things of the Spirit, this is how they reacted:

> *'From that time many of His disciples went back and walked with Him no more.'* (John 6:66)

Jesus ended up with Himself and the twelve. He was not going to compromise the way of the cross in order to get Himself a megachurch.

Have we forgotten God's chosen way of salvation? Through the preaching of the gospel of the cross, God chose to save those who believe. These are the words of the apostle Paul:

> *'For the message of the cross is foolishness to those who are perishing, but to us who are being saved it is the power of God .... For since, in the wisdom of God, the world through wisdom did not know God, it pleased God through the foolishness of the message preached to save those who believe. For Jews request a sign, and Greeks seek after wisdom; but we preach Christ crucified, to the Jews a stumbling block* (an offence) *and to the Greeks foolishness, but to those who are called, both Jews and Greeks, Christ the power of God and the wisdom of God.'* (1 Corinthians 1:18 & 21–24)

God does not want us to change or play about with His way of communicating. We are not to try to modify or adjust the gospel in any way, either because we want to lessen its foolishness, so that people can better understand it, or we want to make it more attractive through a more spectacular presentation. God has closed the message of the cross to the human mind, to human wisdom. We are not to make it less foolish to the mind in order to attract more people, because in doing so we will take away its power. The strange non-comprehensive story about the Son of God being revealed in human flesh, being crucified in utter weakness bearing the sins of the world, being raised triumphantly from the grave by God's power, must stand in all of its foolishness to the human mind. We cannot offer the 'Greeks' of this world any wise explanations. In the same way we cannot offer the 'Jews' of this world some extraordinary and sensational external manifestations to prove the gospel of the cross.

And finally, we are not allowed to change the way the gospel is to be communicated, namely through the preaching of anointed human beings. Let us not forget that the Holy Spirit does not anoint methods, only people. God chose men to speak His Word in order that people could be saved. No show, no performance, no theatre-play and certainly no act of comedians can replace the word being preached by anointed preachers. And those who have abandoned all preaching in their church and replaced it with Christian sing-songs, musicals, and performances of various kinds have taken out the God-ordained way to bring sinners to the cross. We can have all the creative means in the world as helpmates, but we can never abandon the preaching of the foolishness of the message of the cross by anointed vessels, if we want to see real and lasting results of the work of the church.

Enemies of the Cross

How sad Paul felt when he discovered that, among the Philippian Christians there were those who had come away from the centrality of the cross:

> *'For many walk, of whom I have told you often, and now tell you even weeping, that they are the enemies of the cross of Christ; whose end is destruction, whose god is their belly, and whose glory is their shame – who set their mind on earthly things.'* (Philippians 3:18–19)

Paul was weeping when he discovered than some believers had chosen to live their Christian life according to their carnal nature. By doing so they had rejected the crucified life and made satisfaction of their earthly needs and desires the centre of their walk with the Lord. Such cross-less Christianity left the apostle weeping. A message and a life without self-denial. How widespread this 'gospel' has become in the modern church today. All we are taken up with in many places, especially in the western world, is how we can exploit the gospel and the goodness of God for our own gains and needs. And there must be no pain connected to the Word of God any more. We don't like pain. Pain and suffering as an intregal part of our walk with the Lord is being abandoned and replaced with a sugar-sweet message of humanism. It is as if we have forgotten the words of the Master to His disciples:

> *'If anyone desires to come after Me, let Him deny himself, and take up his cross, and follow Me. For whoever desires to save his life will lose it, but whoever loses his life for My sake will find it.'*
>
> (Matthew 16:24–25)

True Christianity is not about strengthening ones self-confidence and self-image. It is about losing self, denying self. And yet we are so concentrated around ourselves. As a matter of fact that is what is so close to our nature: to be occupied with our own needs and our self-image. If that becomes our focus and occupation we develop a cross-less Christianity. Following the Lord and embracing the cross will deliver us from ourselves and enable us to lose and deny ourselves, so that the life of Christ and the power of His resurrection can fill us. But of course the message of the cross is not a popular message, because it brings pain with it into our lives. And pain we do not want. We are by nature always looking for Dr Painless. He was a dentist in a major city in the mid-west of America. He was called that, because he always used an overdose of anaesthetic, so that his patients would feel no pain during his treatment of their teeth. But some treatments were not able to be performed without some pain. So in order to keep up his reputation Dr Painless simply did not perform those operations. For instance he skipped over the deeper root canal operations and only 'fixed' the top. Lots of people flocked to Dr Painless' clinic and received painless treatment. Later of course they discovered to their horror a strong and consistent pain coming from underneath their teeth. A cross-less life can provide us with momentary joy and peace, but in the long run it will destroy our walk with the Lord and in the end cause us eternal damage and pain.

Let us not fall away from the message of the cross and from living the crucified life. Let us take heed to this warning about the days at the coming of the Son of Man by the apostle Paul:

> *'Preach the word! Be ready in season and out of season. Convince, rebuke, exhort, with all long-suffering and teaching. For the time will come when they will not endure sound doctrine, but according to their own desires, because they have itching ears, they will heap up for themselves teachers; and they will turn their ears away from the truth, and be turned aside to fables.'*
>
> (2 Timothy 4:2–4)

We are in that time. Never before have so many of God's people turned away from hard truth, from the realities of God's Word, and given themselves over to wishful thinking and empty spiritual fantasies.

For as in the days of Noah, so shall it be at the coming of the Son of Man.

Chapter 9

When the Fig Tree is Blossoming

'Now learn this parable from the fig tree: When its branch has already become tender and puts forth leaves, you know that summer is near. So you also, when you see all these things, know that it (or He) *is near – at the doors!'* (Matthew 24:32–33)

'Then He spoke to them a parable: "Look at the fig tree, and all the trees. When they are already budding, you see and know for yourselves that summer is now near. So you also, when you see these things happening, know that the kingdom of God is near."'

(Luke 21:29–31)

The word of the Lord Jesus in His great speech about the end of this age exposes many dramatic events as signs of the time of His return to the earth. Most of these signs, yes, in fact all of them except two, represent events and phenomenona that are not new in the history of mankind. Deception has always been around as long as people have inhabited the earth. Wars, famines, pestilences and earthquakes are in no way unfamiliar to human history. Tribulation, persecution and martyrdom of the saints has followed the church since its beginning. Signs in the sky such as mentioned by Jesus have occurred with regular intervals throughout the centuries. There is no doubt however that in the last days before the coming of the Son of Man, all these signs will greatly increase in an unusual manner. Tribulation for instance will be so great,

> '*...such as has not been since the beginning of the world until this time, no, nor ever shall be.*'
> (Matthew 24:21)

And as the Lord Jesus concludes,

> '*...unless those days were shortened, no flesh would be saved, but for the elect's sake those days will be shortened.*' (Matthew 24:22)

And regarding deception, it will be so powerful through false signs and wonders as to deceive *'if possible, even the elect'* (verse 24) – the meaning being that were it not for God's extraordinary divine protection, the whole of the Body of Christ would be led astray. Moral decline has always been a part of human society, but the decline in these last days will be as in the days of Noah, a moral corruption which is totally irreversible and can only be dealt with through utter destruction.

The one exceptional sign which has not previously happened is the completion of the great commission as mentioned in verse 14.

The second one to which we in this chapter devote our attention is the 'budding of the fig tree'. The way Jesus brings up this sign gives you the idea that the thing about the fig tree is the sign which confirms all the other signs. In the context of the fig tree we find these phrases: *'Look at the fig tree, and all the trees'* and *'this generation* (meaning 'this race', namely the Jewish) *will by no means pass away till all things take place.'*

In other words when the fig tree is blossoming, the fig tree being the national symbol of Israel, and at the same time all the other signs are occurring in human history, then we can know for sure, that the Lord Jesus is in fact standing in the door-way. The national rebirth and restoration of Israel is the sign which confirms all the other signs letting us know indeed that we are living in the days of the immediate coming of the Son of Man.

Jesus is furthermore helping us to understand the time by adding this remarkable word:

> *'Heaven and earth will pass away, but My words will by no means pass away.'* (Matthew 24:35)

It is as if the Lord is telling us, that when the great turmoil and upheaval comes that looks like heaven and earth falling apart, then we will see with unmistakable clarity, that the prophetic word of God through His ancient prophets, which we have long time ago forgotten or stopped believing in, will be fulfilled right before our very eyes.

The fig tree has been replanted in its original soil after 2000 years of having been cut down and cast out, because the Lord did not find the fruit He was looking for on it. It was cast away when it rejected its owner, when he came to find fruit on it. In the gospel of Matthew chapter 21 Jesus explains this tragic destiny of the Jewish people in His conversation with His disciples and His discussions with the priests and the pharisees. He uses both an incident with a real fig tree as well as a parable about a vineyard. And in the same chapter preceding these teachings we have this remarkable record of Jesus' entrance into the temple in Jerusalem, where in great anger over the abuse of His Father's House He drives out all the money changers and those who sold doves, and He issues this severe judgement upon the religious leaders of Israel:

> *'My house shall be called a house of prayer, but you have made it a den of thieves.'* (Matthew 21:13)

In other words Israel has fallen away from God's purposes and is no longer serving the living God with true worship. God is not getting the fruit which He expected to have from Israel.

In the parable about the vineyard (Matthew 21:33–43), the landowner (God) is leasing His vineyard (Israel) to some vinedressers (the responsible leadership). At the vintage-time the Landowner sends His servants (His prophets) to the vinedressers to collect the fruit. But the vinedressers take the servants; they beat one, kill one and stone another one. The Landowner sends a new team of servants and they are mistreated the same way. At last He sends His Son. But the vinedressers take the Son and kill Him in order to take over the vineyard. This is a clear reference to the rejection and crucifixion of the Messiah, the Son of God, by the Jewish people. Jesus confirms that by quoting the Scriptures:

> *'The stone which the builders rejected has become the chief cornerstone.'* (Matthew 21:42)

And the conclusion is set forth in the following verse:

> *'Therefore I say to you, the kingdom of God will be taken from you and given to a nation bearing the fruits of it.'* (Matthew 21:43)

This then is pointing to the great transition in God's economy from the old covenant people, Israel, to the new covenant people, the church. And Israel is now slipping out of the limelight, out of the centre of God's attention and His work to fulfil His purposes upon the earth.

But it does not mean that they are out forever. This becomes clear when we consider the incident with the fig tree Jesus cursed, because it had no fruit when He approached it to get something to eat. True, the fig tree withered away when Jesus proclaimed: *'Let no fruit grow on you ever again.'* But from the same story in Mark chapter 11 we learn about an important detail: it withered from the root up. In other words everything that was above the earth withered away and disappeared. However the root was still lying hidden under the ground as an indication that there would come a day when it would once again catch life. There remained a stump which in due time would cause new sprouts to come forth and eventually a new tree to grow up.

The apostle Paul confirms this when in Romans 11 he clearly states that God has not rejected Israel (verse 1). He has set them aside in time and history, but He has not rejected them. *'God has not cast away His people whom He foreknew,'* says Paul, and he then points out that God has a remnant, a stump, through which He will once again bring them back to life, back to the centre of His heart and His purposes on earth. His whole argument in the rest of the chapter is centred around the picture of an olive tree. He argues that the fact that the branches were cut off does not in any way mean that the whole tree is dead. There is still the root left, and one day in God's time the branches that were cut off and thrown away will be grafted into the old tree again. God has in no way finished with the Jewish people. On the contrary, after nearly 2000 years of oblivion and exile He is bringing them back to life and back into His plans and purposes with the world.

When, according to Matthew 24 we have come to the last days, the days of the coming of the Son of Man, the fig tree is back as a resurrected tree with new tender branches and fresh leaves and it is in the process of budding. By this we know that the hour is near for the Son of Man to come, for the Kingdom of God to come!

Notice that there is still no mention of fruit, there is still no evidence of the fig tree bearing fruit. This speaks to us about the fact that Israel in its rebirth and restoration as a nation has not yet entered into its fullness. It still has only branches and leaves, but the fruit is yet to come. Israel is still being formed in the hand of God. She is not yet where God wants her to be, but she is truly under way. The final stage of God's work with Israel, her salvation, her final redemption, the day when all Israel shall be saved, when her blind eyes shall be opened and she shall behold her true Messiah, the Lord Jesus Christ, is still ahead of us. That marvellous event in world history is closely linked with the coming of the Messiah. But the stage has already been set. The platform is being built. Almost all of the preconditions for Israel's redemption have been put in place. The summer is near and soon Israel shall bear those fruits of the kingdom for which God chose her and called her.

The Renewal of Israel

The Prophet Ezekiel gives us God's prophetic agenda for Israel. Chapters 36–39 show us a three-step plan for the renewal of Israel.

The Dry Bones

First we read about the dry bones coming together. This refers to this great and marvellous prophetic event of the Jews returning to the land of their forefathers after two thousand years of exile among the Gentile nations. We call this the second exodus, for this sovereign miracle of God will be of such magnitude, that the miracle of the first exodus out of Egypt will pale into insignificance in comparison, not even worth of mentioning any more:

> *'"Therefore behold, the days are coming," says the Lord, "that it shall no more be said, 'The Lord lives who brought up the children of Israel from the land of Egypt,' but, 'The Lord lives who brought up the children of Israel from the land of the north and from all the lands where He had driven them.' For I will bring them back into their land which I gave to their fathers."'* (Jeremiah 16:14–15)

Unlike the first exodus which brought the Jews out of one nation, Egypt, this second and last one shall bring them back from all the four corners of the earth. And that great move of God is already in full swing. From the land of the north alone, nearly one million Jews have returned to Israel during the last few years. The dry bones are coming together in the land. That they are coming back as 'dry bones' has important meaning for us. God is bringing back to Israel in these days, a people that as a whole are still in spiritual blindness and spiritual death, and just as unbelieving with regard to their Messiah as they were when they rejected Him and were sent into exile. It is very important for us to register this, so that we do not assume that the pre-condition for their return to the holy land is their repentance and turning to their God, and their acceptance of Jesus as their Messiah. God's dealings with the Jewish people do not follow the procedures of church-evangelism. True, they ultimately have to come to repentance and faith in the Messiah like us in order to be saved. For there is no other way to be saved. But God allows Himself the privilege as God to deal with them in His own unique way in order to bring them to the point of salvation. To claim therefore that the Jews must be subjected to the usual way of evangelism for God to work with them is not only a violation of God's sovereignty, but also contradictory to the Scriptures. In the framework of the church we have become so used to centring around the individual in salvation that we have forgotten that God deals with Israel as a nation. Only with reference to Israel do the Scriptures speak about a whole people being born in a day:

> *'Shall the earth be made to give birth in one day? Or shall a nation be born at once? For as soon as Zion was in labour, she gave birth to her children.'* (Isaiah 66:8)

Or take the way the New Testament proclaims it:

> *'And so all Israel will be saved, as it is written: "The Deliverer will come out of Zion, and He will turn away*

> *ungodliness from Jacob; for this is my covenant with them, when I take away their sins."'*
>
> (Romans 11:26–27)

Our attitude and work as the church towards Israel should not be 'evangelistic minded', but we should make ourselves available in prayer and action to co-work with God in bringing back the bones just as dry as they are.

A Body Formed

Once they are back in the land – and since that is an ongoing process over some time, as a simultaneous and parallel work – God is moulding and forming His people into a national body. This is what is meant by this word:

> *'"I will put sinews on you and bring flesh upon you, cover you with skin and put breath in you; and you shall know that I am the Lord." So I prophesied as I was commanded; and as I prophesied, there was a noise, and suddenly a rattling; and the bones came together, bone to bone. Indeed as I looked, the sinews and the flesh came upon them, and the skin covered them over; but there was no breath in them.'* (Ezekiel 37:6–8)

This is the next phase in God's prophetic agenda for the renewal of Israel: to mould and form and build it into a national body with all the facilities and institutions required for its life as a nation. It constitutes another major miracle on God's behalf to bring back a heap of dry bones from all the nations and to join them together into a national skeleton. No wonder that the prophet was hearing the noise of rattling. No wonder that there has been so much noise and fuss about the arrival of a reborn nation called Israel, suddenly emerging as it were from the seas of all peoples. And it is not only the people who are being reborn as a nation, but also the land. That little strip of barren desert which for centuries was nothing more than a haven for desert Bedouins and their flocks of camels and goats, is being transformed into a most fruitful and beautiful garden. Another great miracle when you think about it, but one that is clearly prophesied by the Word of God (Ezekiel 36:30). And then there is of course the rebirth of the Hebrew language as the mother-tongue of modern Israel. A language that had basically been forgotten and buried has suddenly come alive, something that has never happened to any other language in all the history of nations. But still, although no longer just dry bones, there is no spiritual life in the body.

The Redemption of Israel

This is then the third and last phase in this remarkable renewal of the nation of Israel. The spiritual rebirth of Israel, the salvation of all Israel or the redemption of Israel:

> *'For I will take you from among the nations, gather you out of all countries, and bring you into your own land. Then I will sprinkle clean water on you, and you shall be clean; I will cleanse you from all your filthiness and from all your idols. I will give you a new heart and put a new spirit within you; I will take the heart of stone out of your flesh and give you a heart of flesh. I will put My Spirit within you and cause you to walk in My statutes, and you will keep My judgments and do them.'*
>
> (Ezekiel 36:24–27)

> *'Then He said to me, "Prophesy to the breath, prophesy, son of man, and say to the breath, 'Thus says the Lord God: "Come from the four winds, O breath, and breathe on these slain, that they may live."' " So I prophesied as He commanded me, and breath came into them, and they lived, and stood upon their feet, an exceedingly great army.'* (Ezekiel 37:9–10)

So far we have followed the way of renewal for Israel. In the picture of the fig tree we have seen that in the days of the coming of the Son of Man it will be back in the ground, it will have branches and leaves, and it will be budding. But the last and most important thing is still ahead of us: the fruit. This purpose of God for Israel is somehow intertwined and interlinked with the coming of the Messiah.

When Israel enters her last phase in her wonderful restoration, something very unique will take place. The veil of hardening that has blinded her eyes for centuries will suddenly be removed and she will behold that her Messiah is none other than the Lord Jesus, whom she rejected. This will be the glorious redemption taking place when the Holy Spirit is being poured out on the house of Israel:

> *'And I will pour out on the house of David and on the inhabitants of Jerusalem the Spirit of grace and supplication: then they will look on Me whom they pierced. Yes, they will mourn for Him as one mourns for his only son, and grieve for Him as one grieves for a firstborn.'*
> (Zechariah 12:10)

At that moment in history at the time of the coming of the Son of Man, a whole nation shall be born again, all of Israel shall be saved! At that moment Israel shall re-enter fully into God's eternal destiny for her. And the blessed and glorious outcome of her salvation will be enormous and will reach unto the ends of the earth.

According to Paul the entry of the reborn and saved Israel will cause a river of spiritual riches to flow out over the whole world:

> *'Now if their fall is riches for the world, and their failure riches for the Gentiles, how much more their fullness!'* (Romans 11:12)

> *'For if their being cast away is the reconciling of the world, what will their acceptance be but life from the dead?'* (Romans 11:15)

'Life from the dead' – for the whole world! Would it be too much to claim that this means a worldwide revival among the nations? That this salvation of Israel is actually leading to the ultimate fulfilment of Joel's prophecy about God's Spirit being poured out upon all flesh?

Certainly the final entering in of the descendants and children of Abraham into their Messiah will result in the total fulfilment of God's promise to Abraham:

> *'And in you all the families of the earth shall be blessed.'* (Genesis 12:3)

Chapter 10

Israel, God's Chosen Vessel

All God's dealings with the Jewish people, including all His miracles to bring them to Himself in these last days, and into their eternal calling and destiny, is not done for the sake of the Jews themselves. True, God has chosen this people and He loves them, but there is a purpose. He has chosen them as a vessel, as a servant for the fulfilment of His eternal purposes with all mankind, with all the nations, yes, with the whole earth.

When God chose Abraham to leave Ur in Chaldea, it was for a specific purpose that had to do with all of God's creation:

> *'In you all the families of the earth shall be blessed!'*
> (Genesis 12:3)

In choosing Abraham, the father of the Jewish people, God's heart was to bless Abraham and his descendants with the clear view in mind, that he and they should bless all the other nations. God loves all people, all nations, and all of His creation! Thus Abraham and Israel were chosen as God's servant for worldwide blessing.

Actually in the Scriptures God calls Israel for His witness:

> *'"You are My witnesses," says the Lord, "and My servant whom I have chosen, that you may know and believe Me, and understand that I am He."'*
>
> (Isaiah 43:10)

We see here that God has called Israel to Himself that they may come to know Him as God, the only God, the Lord of all. But that is for a purpose:

> *'"I, even I, am the Lord, and besides Me there is no savior ... Therefore you are My witnesses," says the Lord, "that I am God."'* (Isaiah 43:11–12)

Here it is: Israel must come to know the Lord in an intimate and living way, so that they can become living witnesses as to who He is, namely the only true God, the Lord, Creator of heaven and earth.

Israel is there to send a clear and unmistakable message to all the nations upon the earth: the God of Israel is the only God. There is no one besides Him! This then is the true destiny of the Jewish people and it explains its whole history. To be chosen for such a purpose and such a destiny is an awesome thing. It means that you cannot be like all the others. You cannot conform to the normal average standard. Israel cannot be like the other nations, because they are called as a carrier of the nature of God. However much they would like to get away from this calling, God will not allow it. It is this fact which has caused the Jewish people much suffering down through the ages. It is this fact that makes them want to become unchosen. For to be chosen by God means to be separated unto His will and His desires, to be conformed to His character, so that they can be His witnesses to all the nations. As one Jew, who had lost most of his family in the holocaust, said: 'How do I become unchosen?'

It is a far from easy thing to have been chosen by God. Just look at the story about the prophet Jonah. The Lord chose him to go to Nineveh with God's message. But

Jonah would not, because he did not find it in accordance with his religious upbringing to have anything to do with Gentiles. Actually Gentiles were unclean people, and Jewish people were not supposed to mingle with them. It is difficult though, if not impossible, to run away from God's calling, and in Jonah's case we see that God will spare no effort in getting His will through. A tremendous storm and a big fish brought the prophet to his senses and he ended up in Nineveh to do God's work. Jewish history is a long story about a people who constantly sought to get out of God's election and purpose, and for that very reason Jewish history is a story of much suffering.

On the other hand, Jewish history is also a story of nations who entered into much suffering under God's heavy hand in judgement, because they opposed God's way with Israel and crossed His eternal purposes with His chosen people. God says He is willing to give nations as a ransom for the people He has chosen and loves, and men and people for them (Isaiah 43:3–4). In addition there is not a miracle God is not willing to perform in order to get His chosen people through, because He has once and for all made up His mind concerning Israel:

> *'This people I have formed for Myself; they shall declare My praise!'* (Isaiah 43:21)

Even all the sins, rebellion and stubbornness of Israel herself will not prevent or hinder God in achieving His goal. For He has decided to forgive them of all their transgressions and to pour out His Spirit upon them and redeem them and heal them. We can certainly underline here the words of the apostle Paul concerning the Jewish people:

> *'Concerning the gospel they are enemies for your sake, but concerning the election they are beloved for the*

> *sake of the fathers. For the gifts and the calling of God are irrevocable.'* (Romans 11:28–29)

'Irrevocable' means that it cannot be changed, it cannot be taken back. What is done cannot become undone!

Lifting Up a Banner

What is it that the Lord wants to do through Israel? He wants to lift up a banner for all the nations to see. As I said earlier, God wants to send a message to the whole world through His dealings with the Jewish people in these last days. This is what He says:

> *'Behold, I will lift my hand in an oath to the nations, and set up my standard* (banner) *for the peoples.'* (Isaiah 49:22)

Now, what is written upon that banner? Only one thing: *'I, the God of Israel, am the Lord!'* God will let all the nations and all the peoples receive a clear message through Israel, that He is the Lord of both heaven and earth and in complete control of everything.

When the Lord turns in mercy and favour towards the fallen tabernacle of David, this is what His purpose is in doing so:

> *'You will arise and have mercy on Zion; for the time to favor her, yes the set time has come ... So the nations shall fear the name of the Lord, and all the kings of the earth Your glory. For the Lord shall build up Zion; He shall appear in His glory.'* (Psalm 102:13–16)

It is quite clear here. The whole motive in God's heart to rebuild Israel is to let all the nations fear His name and see His glory! The word 'Zion' means in Hebrew 'sign' or 'waymark', which is just another way of saying 'testimony'. The restored Zion shall serve as a mighty testimony about God's greatness and glory.

The word 'banner' is the Hebrew word *'ness'*, which means 'miracle'. When God's great and mighty dealings with Israel take place, there will appear to be miracle upon miracle, one greater than the other. This is God's way of letting the nations know His greatness, power and glory.

This is the real message behind the great miracle God is performing in bringing back the Jewish people from all the nations. Listen to this word from the Lord:

> *'Thus says the Lord God: "I do not do this for your sake, O house of Israel, but for My holy name's sake, which you have profaned among the nations wherever you went. And I will sanctify My great name, which has been profaned among the nations, which you have profaned in their midst; and the nations shall know that I am the Lord," says the Lord God, "when I am hallowed in you before their eyes. For I will take you from among all the nations, gather you out of all countries, and bring you into your own land."'*
>
> (Ezekiel 36:22–24)

For His Name's Sake

There are people who believe that God's dealings with Israel in these last days and the outcome thereof is dependant on the people's response in repentance and obedience to His will. So if the people do not turn to God first, none of His great redeeming acts will ever take effect. These people do not know how wrong they are and how unscriptural they are. They do not understand that God's work is based on grace, and on grace alone. God is not doing all this for Israel for Israel's sake. He is doing it for His own sake!

This is something the Lord tells Israel and us directly:

> *'For my name's sake I will defer My anger, and for My praise I will restrain it from you, so that I do not cut you off . . . For My own sake, for My own sake, I will do it; for how should My name be profaned? And I will not give My glory to another.'* (Isaiah 48:9–11)

There is no doubt whatsoever that Israel has rebelled and sinned against the Lord more than enough for Him to destroy them, to remove them from the face of the earth. But He will not, in fact, actually He cannot. For His holy name is completely tied up with the destiny of Israel, and He cannot allow His name to be profaned among the nations. God has no choice as it were, but to carry it all through against all odds. He has forever linked His very own person with the people He chose to bear His name and to be a witness to who He is. Therein lies a measure of God's grace which goes far beyond what we can think or imagine.

Chapter 11

Great is His Faithfulness

The Jewish people are the greatest evidence of the existence of a living almighty God in the course of human history. They are also manifesting to the world without a shadow of a doubt, that the foremost feature of God's character is His eternal mercy and grace. We can claim without exaggeration, that without God there would be no trace of the Jewish race left on the face of the earth. Their history is so full of suffering, pogroms and holocausts, that if God had not been faithful to His promises to Abraham, Isaac and Jacob, the Jewish people would have disappeared long ago.

The Bible, the Word of God, testifies to that fact in many ways throughout endless crises and tragedies in Jewish life and history.

One such remarkable place in Scripture deals with the prophet Jeremiah, the weeping prophet, as he reflects on the tragedy of the destruction of Jerusalem, when the holy city was turned into rubble by the Babylonian hordes. We find this incident described in the Book of Lamentations. The whole book is basically one big lamentation by Jeremiah over the destruction of Jerusalem. He tells of his own anguish and sorrow over the fact that Jerusalem, which is the symbol of hope and future for all Jewish generations, has now been destroyed. How could God allow this to happen? By this God has failed His people and turned His back on them:

> *'He* (God) *has broken my teeth with gravel, and covered me with ashes. You have removed my soul far from peace; I have forgotten prosperity. And I said, "My strength and my hope have perished from the Lord." Remember my affliction and roaming, the wormwood and the gall. My soul still remembers and sinks within me.'*
>
> (Lamentations 3:16–20)

Jeremiah's heart is filled with despair. He seems to have lost all hope for the future. Everything is dark around him. God has taken away the future of his people by letting the enemy destroy the holy city.

It is in the midst of all this mourning and complaining that something unusual hits the prophet. It is like a big torch that is suddenly turned on, and a beam of great light invades and floods his soul.

The preface to the book describes this remarkable change in this way:

> 'Lamentations describes the funeral of a city. It is a tear-stained portrait of the once proud Jerusalem, now reduced to rubble by the invading Babylonian hordes. In a five-poem dirge, Jeremiah exposes his emotions. A death has occurred; Jerusalem lies barren.
>
> And then, in the midst of this terrible holocaust, Jeremiah triumphantly cries out, "Great is Your faithfulness." In the face of death and destruction, with life seemingly coming apart, Jeremiah turns tragedy into a triumph of faith. God has never failed in the past. God has promised to remain faithful in the future. In the light of the God, he knows and loves, Jeremiah finds hope and comfort.'

The whole wording of this wonderful statement we find in Lamentations 3:22–24:

> *'Through the Lord's mercies we are not consumed, because His compassions fail not. They are new every morning; Great is Your faithfulness. "The Lord is my portion," says my soul, "therefore I hope in Him."'*

This is the story of God's incredible faithfulness towards the Jewish people throughout thousands of years of sufferings and pain. This is the story of their divine calling and destiny which God would never let go of. But this is not only their story. This is also our story and destiny as His New Testament people, as His church.

When everything has been tested and tried; when all there is to say has been said, the reality remains that our only light and only hope is the never failing faithfulness of our Lord God.

In the midst of all human changes, turmoil and failures, it is an enormous encouragement to meditate on this one thought: God can never fail, God can never make a mistake, because He simply cannot change. He is forever the same!

It is only shortly after the writer of the letter to the Hebrews has described the major shakings of heaven and earth, which will take place in the last days (Hebrews 12:26–29), that he makes this awesome proclamation:

> *'Jesus Christ is the same yesterday, today, and forever!'* (Hebrews 13:8)

For us human beings who are changing a lot, it is not easy to understand that there is one person in this wavering and insecure world who never changes, but is always the same:

'Every good gift and every perfect gift is from above, and comes down from the Father of lights, with whom there is no variation or shadow of turning.'

(James 1:17)

As a big contrast to this character of our heavenly Father stands the portrait of an ordinary human person, described earlier in the same chapter as:

'... a wave of the sea driven and tossed by the wind ... a double-minded man, unstable in all his ways.'

(verses 6 & 8)

We as God's people are still here, are still on our way, only because of His great faithfulness. This is true whether we speak about the Old or the New Testament people of God.

In the last book of the Old Testament we find this unusual word spoken by the Lord to His people:

'For I am the Lord, I do not change; therefore you are not consumed, O sons of Jacob. Yet from the days of your fathers you have gone away from My ordinances and have not kept them.' (Malachi 3:6–7)

Here is the altogether reliable fact: He is the Lord, and there is no way He can change! If anyone will have to change, it will have to be us, for God simply cannot change. We should bear this in mind and remember, that there would never be a situation or a circumstance in our life where we could make God change and adjust Himself to our way and our will. No way! I know that there are words in the Bible which seem to indicate that God can change His mind, but we have to be extremely careful to understand this matter correctly. This does not mean that God has changed His original will and purpose in any way. If God did that it would indicate that He was capable of making mistakes, but if that was so, we would never be able to sleep calmly in our beds. No, these words do not refer to any change in God's will and purpose for any cause or any person. What it means, is that God can decide to change the way in which He might accomplish His will and purpose. This happened in God's dealings with the great city of Nineveh. God was going to put His judgement on that wicked city, but when He saw that they responded with repentance, He changed His judgement to revival. The purpose of God stood unchanged, namely that wickedness and sin must be dealt with, but because of the repentance of the inhabitants of Nineveh, God was able to accomplish His will in a way other than He had originally planned.

God never changes. He simply cannot. In the same story about Nineveh, Jonah the prophet opposed God. Did God change? No, Jonah was the one who had to change and adjust his will to God's. That is always the case and will always be the case, for God can make no mistake!

God said: *'I am the Lord, I do not change.'* And this is the blessed fact that led to the rescue and salvation of His people Israel: *'Therefore you are not consumed, O sons of Jacob.'*

Because God cannot change His will, His purpose, His calling, the Jewish people survived nearly 5000 years of turbulent history. They are going to make it and arrive at God's eternal destiny and calling for them, in spite of whatever would seem to get in the way. Whatever schemes the devil will come up with against the Jews in His raging hatred of them, will all fall to the ground. Even in spite of Israel herself and her lack of obedience and submission to God's will for her. Notice that the Lord in this passage calls His people 'sons of Jacob'. He could have called them 'sons of Abraham'; that would have indicated that the people were good people, who believed and obeyed the Lord just like Abraham. Or He could have called them 'sons of Isaac'. Isaac was a wonderful person, gentle, submissive, obedient; he never did anything wrong, and that is why he is used in the Bible as a type of Christ, the Son of God. But no, God characterizes His people here as 'sons of Jacob'. And we all know who Jacob was: the twister, the great manipulator, the worm! The bad guy of the lot, we would say. And that is what the Lord explains in detail by saying:

> *'...from the days of your fathers you have gone away from My ordinances and not kept them!'*

You have been bad company. You have caused Me nothing but problems. You are a real pain in the neck! But in spite of all this: you have not been consumed! Neither by your enemies, and there are plenty of them, nor by your own failures and sins, and there have been plenty of them too.

Neither they, nor we, have been consumed because of one thing alone: God can never change, and great is His faithfulness!

When we look at God's great faithfulness towards Israel we have the assurance that He is the same towards His New Testament people, the church. For if God could fail His old covenant people could He also not fail us? And if He had changed His will and purpose for Israel could it not also happen that He changed His purpose for us, the church?

Thank God, that

> *'Jesus Christ is the same yesterday, today and forever!'*

What is it we put our trust in? How do we think we will be able to make it through to the very end?

It has been written about the well-known missionary to China, Hudson Taylor, who founded the China Inland Mission, that at a certain time in his life, he came to a total end of himself. He had been greatly used by God in China to establish what he called a faith mission, and then in the middle of it all he suffered what today we would call a burn out. Over a period he gradually lost his faith, until in the end he thought of himself as a total failure. He then wrote home to the mission board in England and offered his resignation, telling them in the letter that it had been a mistake for him to be sent out to China. The board alerted all the friends of the mission and much prayer went up for Hudson Taylor. One day some time later, when Hudson Taylor was sitting in his garden in China drinking his afternoon tea, his Bible was lying on the table. Not that he had any intention of reading in it, for the word had not been speaking to him for some time. But that day he put his hand on the book and it fell open almost accidentally on the following word from 2 Timothy 2:13:

> *'If we are faithless, He remains faithful; He cannot deny Himself.'*

The Word hit Hudson Taylor like a hammer, and he realized the great mistake he had make. He had built the mission on faith and had always made a point out of that when he talked about China Inland Mission. But now his faith had disappeared and the mission had come to a stand still. Through this word the Lord completely restored his servant, but from that day on Hudson Taylor stopped talking about CIM as being a faith mission. Now, he said, it had become a work firmly founded on God's faithfulness and not on anybody's faith. For if we should lose our faith, our energy and strength, our vision and hope, God would still be there with all His resources on full. For if we are without faith, God is still full of faith, for He cannot deny Himself!

If He has called us whether as His Israel or His church, we can rest assured that He is going to bring us through to our divine destination, for:

> *'He who calls you is faithful, who will also do it.'*
> (2 Thessalonians 5:24)

'For the gifts and calling of God are irrevocable.'
(Romans 11:29)

Great is His faithfulness!

Chapter 12

The Overcoming Church

In the days of the coming of the Son of Man there are many exciting things happening, which we have considered in this book. The great commission is being completed, the fig tree, the nation of Israel, is being restored and we are looking forward with great expectation to the soon coming of our glorious King and Messiah. However this last bit of the way will always mean growing pressures and persecution against the people of God. Anti-semitism and anti-christianity will increase as Satan mobilises all his forces in a last attempt to gather together the nations of the world in rebellion against the Lord.

This is also clearly pointed put by the Lord Jesus in His great speech in Matthew 24:

> *'All these are the beginning of sorrows. Then they will deliver you up to tribulation and kill you, and you will be hated by all nations for My name's sake. And then many will be offended, will betray one another, and will hate one another. Then many false prophets will rise up and deceive many. And because lawlessness will abound, the love of many will grow cold. But he who endures to the end shall be saved.'* (Matthew 24:8–13)

In other words: there will be increasing pressures and hardships for God's people in the days of the coming of the Son of Man. And also we should not forget that in addition to these problems, God's people will of course also be hit by what Jesus here calls 'sorrows', meaning the physical shakings of nature and of the world. We will have to share in the sufferings following earthquakes, famines, diseases and wars with the rest of mankind, as truly as we share in human life here on the earth.

The idea that God would somehow take us away before the first shot has been fired in the end-time battle, I find very hard to prove biblically, although I certainly would like to believe it would be like that. But such an idea in my estimation is more out of wishful thinking that of biblical reality. If we would not have to encounter at least part of the end-time shakings it would not make any sense when Jesus in Matthew 24 prepares us for persecutions, betrayals, and that even some of us will be killed. Nor would He warn us of such powerful deception coming against us, that if God did not put a stop to it, we would all fall under its power. Also if we as God's children will be taken up in the rapture before the hard and tough times occur, would there be any reason for the great falling away?

Surely we shall have our part of the 'sorrows', although I totally agree with those who say that we will be raptured before God pours out His wrath upon the earth. The Lord is not however warning us about these trials in order to discourage us or depress us. On the contrary He encourages us to lift up our head when the sorrows begin to come, because He wants us to look beyond a short time of darkness and fix our eyes upon the bright light which will follow. He does not want us to focus on the night, but rather that we turn our eyes towards the dawn which surely will follow the night's darkness and gloom. It is to that end the Lord Jesus gives us this exhortation:

> *'Now when these things begin to happen, look up and lift up your heads, because your redemption draws near.'* (Luke 21:28)

The Lord wants us to understand that the shaking of heaven and earth is God's doing with a clear redemptive purpose. Just as it always is with God's judgements. They are implemented upon the earth in order to remove wickedness and make a way for God's purposes to be realized. This is the reason why the word 'sorrows' can also be translated 'birth pangs' indicating that through this time of dreadful pain and suffering something beautiful and wonderful is going to be born. It is a hard time for the pregnant woman when the birth pangs start moving in her body, and surely she does not like this period at all, but when after a while the baby is born, her heart is filled with joy and happiness. The moment she holds her new born baby in her arms, she has already forgotten all about the birth pangs. So we must try to look up, to look away through the tribulation and the pain and unto the great birthing of the kingdom of God which the Lord Jesus will bring in upon the earth at His soon and glorious coming!

The Lord also points out, that at this severe and difficult time in history at the coming of the Son of Man, a unique opportunity will be given to His church to bring the word of the gospel to people around us. And He encourages us not be worried about how to fulfil our ministry in those days:

> *'...you will be brought before kings and rulers for My name's sake. But it will turn out for you as an occasion for testimony. Therefore settle it in your heart not to meditate beforehand on what you will answer, for I will give you a mouth and wisdom which all your adversaries will not be able to contradict or resist.'*
>
> (Luke 21:12–15)

What a glorious time that will be for bringing God's love and His word to people's hearts, which are

> *'...failing them from fear and the expectation of those things which are coming on the earth.'* (Luke 21:26)

And how wonderful that we need not worry ahead of time about what to say and how to do it. God will provide what we need; not ahead of time, but when we need it.

Having an Ear to Hear

There is so much anxiety among Christians about how to prepare for this time of trouble. We hear about some who are trying to secure their finances or double their life insurances. There are even those who try to prepare physically by storing up canned food in nuclear-safe shelters. This kind of preparation is of little value and most often a waste of time. We cannot store up money, nor provisions, and we cannot protect ourselves by building shelters. The worth of money could and most likely will, crash overnight, and our insurances would not be worth the paper they are written on. And there is no 'safe' place or building where we could hide away to avoid the trouble. The only safety there is is in the perfect will of God. Safety is of the Lord, and only of Him!

When the land of Israel was hit by famine in the time of Elijah, his only way of survival was his ability to hear the voice of the Lord:

> *'Get away from here and turn eastward, and hide by the brook Cherith, which flows into the Jordan. And it will be that you shall drink from the brook, and I have commanded the ravens to feed you there.'*
>
> (1 Kings 17:3–4)

How remarkable! Elijah could never ever have figured out that this would be the way to overcome in the time of the famine, to drink from a little brook far away and to be fed by the birds of heaven. God knows how to take care of His children in times of great crisis. But we need to be able to hear His voice and follow His directions. And after the little brook ran dry of water, God had prepared a widow in Zarephath, who had a little oil and a handful of flour stored away, through which the Lord could multiply enough bread for the prophet, the widow and her son.

To be able to overcome in the end-time trouble, our primary need is to be able to hear from God. God's protection and His provision for us will depend on having an ear to hear. All our accumulated knowledge and wisdom will not help us, and all of our own preparation relying on our own strength and intellect will basically be a waste of time.

In His seven messages to seven churches in Minor Asia, as recorded in Revelation chapters 2 and 3, the Lord Jesus repeats two things in every letter which seem to be interlinked:

> *'He who has an ear, let him hear what the Spirit is saying to the churches . . . '*

and

> *'He who overcomes, will I give . . . '*

Overcoming whatever we as God's people will face in these last days will depend on our ability to hear the voice of the Holy Spirit. We Pentecostal, charismatic people who always claim to have the fullness of the Spirit, often have great difficulties in hearing from God, because we focus on and get stuck in the external manifestations of the Spirit. Here we can learn another lesson from the life of Elijah. After his great victory for the Lord on Mount Carmel, where he killed the 400 false prophets of Baal and proved that the God of Israel is God alone, he fled into the desert afraid of the threats of a woman, Jezebel, the queen. He was hiding away in fear and complained to the Lord, and the Lord revealed Himself to Elijah and met with him there. This is the word of the Lord to Elijah:

> *' "Go out, and stand on the mountain before the Lord." And behold, the Lord passed by, and a great and strong*

> *wind tore into the mountains and broke the rocks in pieces before the Lord, but the Lord was not in the wind; and after the wind an earthquake, but the Lord was not in the earthquake; and after the earthquake a fire, but the Lord was not in the fire; and after the fire a still small voice* (or a delicate whispering voice).*'*
>
> (1 Kings 19:11–12)

Of course when the Almighty and powerful God moves there is often some spectacular manifestation to go with it, but God is not in them. God is in that small still voice of the Spirit whispering His word into our spirit. If we do not come to the point where we hear that voice and receive the message, we have missed God, even as we revel in all the power-stuff that moves with Him. The question we must ask ourselves in any encounter with God is this: Did we hear His voice? Did we receive His message? Because if there was no word or no message we never really touched God. We just flowed in the power-charged peripherals. The problem we face in today's church is our great hunger for power. We are chasing around in the global Body of Christ to find power. We have become 'power-minded'. In many places it is all about 'power-evangelism', 'power-healing', 'power-praying' and 'power-worship'. But the crucial issue and the one which decides if we have really met with God is whether we have heard His voice and received His message.

Seeking His Face

But how can we ever hear God's voice unless we seek intimate fellowship with the Lord and learn to dwell in His presence? The reason why Elijah was able to hear from God, was the fact that he had positioned himself in His presence. Again and again Elijah gives this testimony:

> *'As the Lord God of Israel lives, before whom I stand.'*
>
> (1 Kings 17:1)

If we want to prepare ourselves in a real and true way, we should practice, develop and increase our intimacy with God. It is in that intimate fellowship with God that we have rest and protection, provision and guidance through the deep waters. Our lives are often poor and weak spiritually because we have not understood that we need to stay close to the Lord all the time:

> *'Blessed is the man . . . whose delight is in the law of the Lord, and in His law he meditates day and night. He shall be like a tree planted by the rivers of water, that brings forth its fruit in its season, whose leaf also shall not wither; and whatever he does shall prosper.'*
> (Psalm 1:2–3)

The secret of such a man's victory in life is his on-going focus on the Lord and his constant communication with Him. His roots are deep into Christ, the living water, and he draws from Him all he needs.

The Book of Jeremiah links this picture of the tree planted by the water, to the very subject we are talking about here, namely how we can overcome in the time of great heat and upheaval:

> *'Blessed is the man who trusts in the Lord, and whose hope is the Lord. For he shall be like a tree planted by the waters, which spreads out its roots by the river, and will not fear when heat comes; but its leaf will be green, and will not be anxious in the year of drought, nor will cease from yielding fruit.'* (Jeremiah 17:7–8)

When our roots go deep down into Christ, we shall not be affected by the heat or the drought which is on its way in the last days. We must learn to stretch down into Christ, for He is our only hiding place and our only provision. This is what we are exhorted to do by the apostle Paul:

> *'As you therefore have received Christ Jesus the Lord, so walk in Him, rooted and built up in Him . . . For in Him dwells all the fulness of the Godhead bodily.'*
>
> (Colossians 2:6–7 & 9)

We must learn to live out of the roots as they grow down further and further into the underground moisture and water, and to draw from the inner water-fountain in Christ, instead of relying on external watering by the sporadic rainfalls. Many years ago this came home to me in a way that I will never forget. I visited a friend's house on a hot and dry summer's day. Actually we were in a week-long period of a drought. So my friend was busy watering the trees and plants in his garden through a hose. When we walked around the garden and talked as he watered his plants, I noticed that he jumped over a small bush growing alongside the wall of his house. The soil around that little bush was totally dry and the sun burned against it. In my surprise I turned to my friend and told him that he had forgotten the little bush. 'No', he said, 'I did not forget to water it, and I have no intention of doing so, for I do not want to kill the bush.' And then he explained to me that he had brought home this particular bush from the Middle East, where it normally grows in desert areas, where there is no rainfall. 'If I make it a habit to water this plant', he further explained, 'it will stop growing its roots, stretching them deeper and deeper down into the underground water supply, and then when I go away on holidays for weeks and come home again, I would find my little precious bush withered and dead.' What a lesson for us to learn. We too need to grow our roots into Christ and learn to draw from His life within, instead of looking to whatever spiritual water we can get from various charismatic rainfalls.

This is David's secret, the man after God's own heart, who so often was thrown into times of trial and tribulation:

> *'One thing have I desired of the Lord, that will I seek; that I may dwell in the house of the Lord all the days of my life, to behold the beauty of the Lord, and to inquire in His temple. For in the time of trouble He shall hide me in His pavilion; in the secret place of His tabernacle He shall hide me; He shall set me high upon a rock. And now my head shall be lifted up above my enemies all around me; therefore I will offer sacrifices of joy in His tabernacle; I will sing, yes, I will sing praises to the Lord.'* (Psalm 27:4–6)

When our lives are truly *'hidden with Christ in God'* (Colossians 3:3) we shall be able to stand and to overcome all enemies and all calamities in the last days, the days of the coming of the Son of Man.

Watch and Pray

As we desire to come closer to the Lord, to enter into intimate fellowship with Him, we will find that the way is to be devoted to prayer. God gave us the mystery of prayer to be able to communicate with Him.

In the last days, the days of the coming of the Son of Man, prayer becomes a high priority in order for us to be overcomers. The apostle Peter underlines the importance of prayer in the end-time in this way:

> *'But the end of all things is at hand; therefore be serious and watchful in your prayers.'* (1 Peter 4:7)

Prayer is the only real and appropriate answer to the end-time crisis that enables us to stand up to the situation.

Jesus actually concludes His great end-time message with a solemn call to prayer:

> *'But take heed to yourselves, lest your hearts be weighed down with carousing* (dissipation), *drunkenness, and cares of this life, and that Day come on you*

> *unexpectedly. For it will come as a snare on all those who dwell on the face of the whole earth. Watch therefore, and pray always that you may be counted worthy to escape all these things that will come to pass, and to stand before the Son of Man.'* (Luke 21:34–36)

Here it is said loud and clear by the Lord Himself, that without a life of prayer we do not stand a chance to escape all the dangers and temptations of the last days. We have no weapon, no protection against the powers of deception and temptation and fear and anxiety which will fill the air we breathe as a thick cloud of poison in the last days, unless we are fully and wholly committed to seek God in prayer. And when one sees how little the modern church emphasises prayer, one gets genuinely concerned for the future of God's people. The traditional programs of church activities will not do it. If we want seriously to prepare ourselves to come through the time ahead of us victoriously, we must cancel our programs and give ourselves to seek God's face in earnest prayer. We must not only pray more than we do; we must make prayer the absolute highest priority as individuals as well as the church. This is the only way according to Jesus in which we can avoid being trapped in the snare that is coming upon the whole earth.

The warning of the Lord to His people was: *'He who endures to the end shall be saved.'* Now, the word 'saved' here does not mean our eternal life. We do not have eternal life because we endure or deliver any other effort to God. Eternal life is a gift of grace. To be saved in the meaning used in Matthew 24:13 cannot mean that if we do not endure the tribulation we will lose eternal life, and not end up in heaven. No, it means that if we do not endure we will not be able to go through the hard times victoriously but will fall victim to some of the powers of evil and will have to compromise. This is not only a theoretical possibility, but judging from the words of Jesus most likely the majority of Christians will not be able to stand their ground. We learn that from the word 'many' used so often in Jesus's speech: *'Many will be offended, will betray one another and will hate one another, ... many false prophets will ... deceive many'*, and *'the love of many will grow cold.'* Whether we like it or not we must understand that according to God's Word many will fall away in the last days. To try to ignore this fact can in the end prove to be disastrous. The Word of God is unmistakably clear:

> *'Let no one deceive you by any means; for that Day will not come unless the falling away comes first.'*
> (2 Thessalonians 2:3)

The only real defense God offers His people is to be able to escape the trap and the snare by watching and praying.

When Jesus went into the garden of Gethsemane to pray and went through His great agony and pain as He prepared Himself to go to the cross, He took His disciples Peter, James and John with Him. He was seeking their fellowship and support:

> *'"My soul is exceedingly sorrowful, even to death. Stay here and watch with Me," He said to them.'*
> (Matthew 26:38)

But they were overcome by sleep, and Jesus when He came back found them sleeping. It was in that situation Jesus spoke these tremendously important words:

> *'Watch and pray, lest you enter into temptation. The spirit indeed is willing, but the flesh is weak.'*
> (Matthew 26:41)

Without watching and praying we will not be able to overcome the satanic pressures but will fall victim to his subtle traps and temptations.

Only a praying church can be an overcoming church in the days of the coming of the Son of man.

> *'The end of all things is at hand; therefore be serious and watchful in your prayers.'* (1 Peter 4:7)

If you have enjoyed this book and would like to help us to send a copy of it and many other titles to needy pastors in the **Third World**, please write for further information or send your gift to:

Sovereign World Trust
PO Box 777, Tonbridge
Kent TN11 0ZS
United Kingdom

or to the **'Sovereign World'** distributor in your country.